DIGGING
DITCHES

DIGGING DITCHES

Helen Roseveare

CHRISTIAN FOCUS

© Copyright Helen Roseveare 2005

ISBN 1-84550-058-X

10 9 8 7 6 5 4 3 2

Published in 2005
by
Christian Focus Publications, Ltd.,
Geanies House, Fearn, Tain,
Ross-shire, IV20 1TW, Scotland
and
WEC International,
Bulstrode, Oxford Road, Gerrards Cross,
Bucks, SL9 8SZ

www.christianfocus.com

Printed and bound by
CPD, Wales

Cover Design by Alister MacInnes

Contents

Prologue

~~~~~~

'Make this valley full of ditches!'

The words almost sprang out of the page – I knew God had spoken. But did I really want to hear? I had asked him to give me just such a clear word, a 'Thus saith the Lord' type of word, to guide me into the next stage of my journey. But now that He had spoken, I was almost afraid to hear His voice.

I was lying in a hospital bed, following two major operations within a week. I had just completed a nine-month tour of deputation meetings in the USA for my Mission (WEC International) following 20 years of missionary service in Congo. Halfway through that tour, which included over 400 public meetings (school assemblies, church youth groups and Sunday services, university Christian Unions and women's meetings), in over 20 different states, as well as six weeks in Canada, I found that I had a lump (a tumour). It was early in February, a Thursday morning of a busy week. I managed to control my thoughts and go ahead with the meetings already arranged for that day and the following. Saturday was a free day to prepare for several engagements on the Sunday and during the coming week. I asked my host and hostess if they would be kind enough to leave me on my own for a while. I knew I had to find peace in my own heart to continue the tour, knowing that medically, others would consider that I should go for help. I was very conscious that if I backed out, and asked to go home for treatment, it would cause enormous difficulties for those who arranged the tour. The publicity, arrangements for meetings, transport and hospitality for the whole four months would be thrown into confusion.

That Saturday morning, 7th February 1976, I read my morning portion from the Scriptures, then I read Daily Light and prayed. I simply laid it all before the Lord. What did He want me to do? As I re-read the Scripture passage, I sensed God speaking His peace into my heart. Reading through the Bible in a year, I had reached Exodus 1 to 3 that morning. Many years before, God had spoken to me clearly through Exodus 2:9, when Pharaoh's daughter charged the mother of the baby Moses, found in a basket in the reeds at the river's edge, to care for the baby – her own baby! – with the promise: '*Take this baby and nurse him for me, and I will pay you (I will give you your wages).*'

In 1954, when I had been in Congo (at that time, the Belgian Congo) just sixteen months, the Mission Committee asked me to move our fledgling medical programme from Ibambi to Nebobongo, a then disused leprosy colony seven miles up the road. I was terrified at the mere thought of what such a move would mean – all the responsibility of developing the village, as well as starting again all that was involved in developing a health service. I felt angry with that committee, feeling they had been thoughtless towards me, and I almost rebelled. Seeking the Lord's direction at that time, my morning reading had been in Exodus chapter 2. And the Lord said, 'This fledgling health service is your baby. Take it, and care for it in My Name, and I will see that you lack for nothing of which you have need.' I moved out on that promise, and the Lord never failed me through the many turbulent years that followed.

Now, was He saying to me, 'I have a new baby to entrust to you. Will you trust Me?' Then I turned back to read again the verses in Daily Light for the 7th February, and I read: '*One of them, when he saw that he was healed, turned back and with a loud voice, glorified God, and fell down on his face at His feet, giving Him thanks: and he was a Samaritan. And Jesus said:*

'Were there not ten cleansed? but where are the nine? There are not found that returned to give glory to God, save this stranger.' (Lk.17:15- 18 KJV)

I looked up the passage in my Bible and read the following verse, which said: *'Jesus said to him, "Rise and go; your faith has made you well'* (Lk. 17:19 KJV). It was all part of the story of ten leprous men who came to Jesus for healing. All ten had been *healed*, but just one turned back to thank the Lord for His healing, and that one was made *whole* by faith, and through giving thanks. In my heart, I knew that God was speaking to me, into my immediate situation, and I accepted, understanding that I was to continue with all the tour of meetings, to say nothing to anyone of what I feared to be going on in my body, and, actually, to think no more about it for the time being. In other words, God would look after my need for physical healing, but, more immediately, He would give me spiritual wholeness as I trusted and thanked him. He would indeed 'pay my wages' each step of the way ahead.

I rejoined my host and hostess later that morning with peace in my heart and was enabled to accept the first two of God's challenges, even if I did not manage to think no more about it! Two months later in the tour, when taking a week of meetings among university students in Chicago, I became feverish and unable to keep any food down. My mind worked overtime and I presumed that I had secondaries from the rapidly growing lump. This did not prove to be the case and I probably had a sharp attack of 'flu. I was enabled to keep almost all my engagements, despite two weeks of feeling rotten and very weak. Eventually the tour ended and I returned to the UK, where I rang my brother-in-law, the medical superintendent of a general hospital in the west of England. A medical check-up resulted in immediate admittance to hospital and then surgery. Initially thought to be benign, a simple local excision was carried out. But further laboratory sectioning confirmed that there were malignant cells present. So three days after the first, I underwent a second operation.

I was now recovering. What had the Lord for me? Would I really recover, or merely have a few more years in which to serve Him on earth? What could I do for the Lord in that time? What was His plan for my life? I was not unduly worried. I had had four months to accustom myself to the situation. In fact, I had already begun to think in terms of a three-year appointment to a job that I felt I could manage, so as to be fully occupied in the Lord's service as long as I had strength to do it. After that... well, I was willing to wait till that time came and trust Him to see me through any difficult years that followed. I actually wrote to the missionary team in Congo, when I first knew I had a lump and that I might not have much more time to serve the people, to suggest that perhaps they would give me the privilege of going back to them to serve in a new capacity, training African pastors, using French as the medium for teaching rather than Swahili, so that they would be more highly regarded by the authorities. I received no answer to my letter.

After coming round from the anaesthetic, I asked a nurse to open my Bible for me at the marker, and to prop it up on the bed table. I prayed, and asked the Lord to speak to me very clearly. Then I saw that the marker was at 2 Kings 3. How could God ever speak to me, in a meaningful way, through that Old Testament passage? I knew the story. I had taught it at the students' college in Congo not so very long before.

'Lord,' I prayed, 'I really need a "Thus saith the Lord" so that I can stand on Your Word for the next stage of my life.'

However, despite my doubts, I started to read. The chapter relates how, following the refusal of the Moabites to pay the annual tribute they owed to King Joram of Israel, he joined forces with the kings of Judah and Edom and marched south, presumably along the western border of the Dead Sea, to come round to the southern end of the territory of Moab, in order to attack the Moabites, hoping to take them by surprise. When the combined armies reached the River Arnon, expecting to refill all their exhausted water supplies, they found only a dried-up river-bed! The soldiers were ready for mutiny. The three kings, having discussed the situation, called for the prophet Elisha and told him to ask his God what they should do in this emergency.

The Spirit of God came upon Elisha, and God spoke to him: *'Make this valley full of ditches.'* Furthermore, God told him that although they would neither hear wind nor see rain, He would fill the ditches in the valley with water.

That verse, *'**Make this valley full of ditches**'* started with the words, *'**Thus saith the Lord.**'* or in the modern version: *'This is what the Lord says.'*

As my eyes moved down the page, and as I approached verse 16, I stopped and prayed that the Lord would make me willing to hear what He wanted to say to me. I was scared. I knew the story, and now I could see a 'Thus saith the Lord' coming. What would it mean for me?

As soon as I read it, even without going on to read the rest of the story: how the soldiers did as God said, and made the whole sandy river-bed full of ditches; how, during the night, God filled the ditches with water; how, in the early morning light, the Moabite army on the mountain-top to the north saw the rising sun reflected in the water and, presuming the ditches to be filled with blood from fighting between the Israeli and Judaean soldiers; how they had swarmed down the mountainside to plunder the camp, and how the Israelite and Judaean armies fell on them and brought about a resounding victory. I knew that God had spoken to me.

*'**Make this valley full of ditches.**'*

'This valley' must mean the present circumstances of my life, and so much had happened that year. My dear mother had died. I had just completed an exhausting nine months of touring and speaking in the USA and Canada. That week I had had surgery for cancer. It seemed unlikely that WEC would allow me back to the mission field, at least initially. Life felt very uncertain. It was indeed a valley situation.

'Make .. it .. full of ***ditches***.' I was not being asked to dig a Suez Canal, just a multitude of small ditches, each one individually important. Was God asking me to live a day at a time, and do each small task as it arose without asking for one long-term goal? Those soldiers, in the Bible narrative, could have revolted and refused to dig mere ditches. 'It's not what we trained for! We have no proper tools! It's beneath our dignity!' But in fact, they appeared to have obeyed. Of course, without the ditches the water that God wanted to send would have been wasted; it would have soaked without trace into the sandy riverbed. The ditches were essential to contain the promised blessing.

If God asked me to do tasks for which I felt I wasn't trained, tasks that appeared to be much less strategic than all that had been achieved in the past twenty years of medical service in the Congo, was I willing to trust Him and go ahead, one step at a time, doing whatever He chose to ask of me, day by day, even without any apparent long-term goal?

Suddenly it all seemed very insecure. For twelve years, as director of a small hospital in the great Congolese forest land, I had had a clear-cut daily programme, well-defined responsibilities, a measurable task for which I was accountable. Again, in later years, as director of a college for African paramedical workers, my job had had clear limits, a specific goal, a tidy programme. Even when I first came home to help care for my invalid mother, there had been a regular daily programme, and others had always been available to help as needed. But now, the box in which I felt God was asking me to live seemed very open-ended. To whom would I be accountable? How would I know, each day, just what was asked of me? Would I be financially supported? Hundreds of questions raced through my mind, yet the Lord's words were clear and unequivocal: *'Make this valley full of ditches'* **and**, with the command, came the promise: *'This valley will be filled with water!'* He enabled me to say, 'OK, yes, Lord!'

For many years after I became a Christian, I yearned for the mountain-tops, for experiences of God's glory and power, of His enabling and blessing. The story of Caleb (in Joshua 14:6-14), who, at the age of 80, asked Joshua to give him the hill country as his inheritance, despite all the savage inhabitants and obvious difficulties, stirred me. Caleb was said to have followed the Lord wholeheartedly. That was what I wanted to do. Caleb was sure God would give him all the victory he needed to achieve his goal, and I knew I wanted to trust the Lord in the same way. Basically, I wanted to live on the Mount of Transfiguration!

During the first twelve years at Nebobongo, we watched God do some amazing things. The small village had grown up and expanded around the church. Pastor Agoya, and his wife Taadi, worked tirelessly amongst the nursing students, the hospital patients and their relatives. Yandibio transformed the primary school, teaching some 170 children in four grades. Mama Damaris cared for orphaned babies with endless love and patience. Mangadima and I trained twelve male students every year to be paramedical workers who carried the main load of an ever-expanding hospital. When qualified, they staffed some ten small rural hospitals and forty or fifty dispensaries and clinics. Thousands of patients were treated every year, hundreds undergoing urgently needed surgical interventions. Mud and thatch buildings were slowly replaced by brick ones with permanent roofing. All our young people became enthusiastic members of our Campaigner Clan. Students played football with energy (even if not with a great deal of knowledge of rules!) and all ages joined together in a church choir.

We were a happy family. God graciously sent revival into our midst during the early years together, and that cemented our relationships one with another. There was little or no consciousness of colour differences. We shared all we had and grew together spiritually through many difficulties and frustrations, as well as through the good times.

It is true that there were some gravely ill patients whom we could not help, empty shops that could not provide needed building or school supplies, a broken down truck that taxed our ingenuity to keep it on the road. There was always the urgent need to respect the national people and their customs, whilst seeking to train them in good medical practice, and the urgent need to understand and keep industrial law as we handled workmen and nurses, on minimal finances. Then there was the urgent need to keep healthy, despite carrying an enormous workload and heavy responsibilities. Yes, there *were* difficulties and frustrations, and so many urgent needs. But we grew spiritually through them all, and the times of joy and blessing outweighed the problem times.

In 1960, handing over control of the country from Belgian officials to Congolese nationals caused enormous hardships and much misunderstanding. Foreigners were often barely tolerated. All leadership needed to be passed to nationals, even when there was no-one trained to carry such responsibility. There was mutiny in the national Congolese army, a breakdown of all communications, emptying shops and an almost total lack of supplies of food or medicines. Yet we worked our way through another four years of mounting difficulties, and God once again wonderfully undertook for us.

Suddenly, in 1964, we were engulfed in civil war. Guerrilla soldiers took over and cruelty reigned. Thousands were killed senselessly. Infrastructure was needlessly destroyed. Schools had to close. Hospitals could hardly cope with the influx of the seriously wounded, with minimal stocks of anaesthetics or antibiotics. Yet through the whole 18 months of mindless tyranny, the church grew. Many congregations more than doubled! Christians took every opportunity to share the gospel with terrified villagers and marauding soldiers alike. 'How is it you are not afraid?' they were often asked, by the amazed population. And they were quick to share the Good News of Jesus Christ on each occasion.

After five months of captivity I, along with most other missionaries in our area, were rescued and flown to our home countries to recover. During the ensuing 14 months, I wrote *Give me this mountain*, the first part of my autobiography, that tells my story up to that moment in 1965. And the discipline of writing helped to clear my heart and mind of the trauma of the months of captivity.

At last, news trickled out that the national army, strengthened by fifty mercenary soldiers (mostly from South Africa), were liberating our area. Peace was slowly being restored and letters began to come to us from our local African leaders. Would we ever consider going back to help them recover from the devastation? It was so thrilling to realise that they *wanted* us back, that the way was opening up to make our return possible. We heard that 'everything' had been destroyed: buildings, equipment, supplies, hospital, schools and homes. We hoped they were exaggerating. Could we face the mammoth task of reconstruction, knowing that it could all happen again? My excitement became tinged with doubts. Could I mentally and spiritually stand up to the strain of all that would be involved in returning? Had I known all that the next seven years would include, I might well have chosen not to go. But God mercifully hid the details from our eyes! And He filled us with His peace and the assurance of His protection as we returned.

During those 14 months at home the Lord started to re-focus my heart from the ever-deep desire to live on the mountain-tops, to the realisation that God's work is mostly done in the valleys, doubtless spurred on by the vision given on the mountain but, in practice, turning that vision into reality in the valley. When we returned to Congo in 1966, we found the rumours were basically true. Rebel forces *had* destroyed 90 percent of all we had built at Nebobongo in the previous twelve years. It was clear that we would have to re-build and start all over again. But then came the surprising direction to leave Nebobongo and go 450 miles to the east, to re-start the work in the valley at Nyankunde.

At Nyankunde, on the foothills of the Ruwenzori mountains, above the treeline and out of the endless forest, there were huge views and a much better climate. Five missionary societies agreed to join forces and start a new, larger, better-equipped hospital, with a Government-recognised college to train national medical and paramedical workers. Dr Carl Becker, a seasoned Africa Inland Mission (AIM) missionary, and I had dreamed of such a joint venture for several years. Suddenly, it was as though the civil war with all its destruction had precipitated a fulfilment of the vision. Dr Becker would run the hospital and the multiple medical services that would be involved, and I would run the training college. The team grew around us. Three or four other doctors joined us, several American and Swiss nurses, and eventually one other English nurse/midwife tutor. The Government encouraged us to go ahead and develop the work, though no-one was willing to put their signature to an official document! Richard Dix and his team made bricks and put up buildings. Dr Becker and his team saw and treated nearly 1,000 outpatients every day. And I, with a small team, taught student boys from all over the north-east of Congo and Rwanda to become the medical-evangelists that were so urgently needed. But this did not happen overnight!

The land we were given was an overgrown valley, rough brambles and wild elephant grasses growing out of a thick layer of black mud! Dr Becker had his vision already fairly clearly in his mind and heart. Waving his hand up the valley he told me I could have some four to five acres of it to develop the college. I paced it all out, stuck flags in the four corners then clambered up the hillside and looked down on 'my' valley and asked God to give me a vision of the college rather than just a vision of a valley full of mud. By modern radio and ancient bush-telegraph, we sent out messages to invite students, both men and women, who had finished at least one year of secondary school education, and who had a desire to serve the population in medical work, to turn up. The first group arrived in early August 1966 – expectant, yet also suspicious. Some were proud and a little disdainful, others were shy and a little fearful.

Where was the college they had come to join? 'Over there,' I answered, as nonchalantly as I could manage, waving an arm up the mountain slopes. And the dormitories? 'Also there,' I declared. As they realised that there was no college and no dormitories... 'You build, I'll teach!' I challenged them. It took them 24 hours to take in my preposterous suggestion that they should take their shirts off, clear and weed, dig and shovel, cut down trees, build, roof and thatch their own school, village, classrooms, dining hall and dormitories. But eventually they agreed, and together we did it. In October 1966, we started classes. Two years later, and every year afterwards, a group entered for Government exams, passed, and were awarded the coveted certificates.

Of course, during the next seven years, there were exasperating situations, when students pitted their strength against mine. They wanted better meals. 'OK, provide your own!' I told them. They wanted better subsidies for their fees. 'OK, I'll withdraw what I put in every week, and you can find your own!' Once or twice, the rebellion was more serious, and it took all our skill and prayers to bring them round to accept God's discipline, as well as His love and grace. There were frustrations, as when the needed roofing nails did not come in time to complete the roof before the rainy season started, and when paint eventually arrived from the 'city', some 500 miles west, with three of the twelve tins filled with water. But slowly, our valley turned into a well-respected, Government-accepted college. Our vision became a reality.

Then I began to realise that I owed it to my brother and younger sisters – all married with teenage children – to take my share of the responsibility of caring for our dear mother. At the same time, my own physical strength was severely tested by several bouts of tropical fevers. Besides that, my nervous energy was running low, so often tested as it was by mindless bureaucracy or sometimes brutal harassment. The Trades' Union was always ready to pounce and cause unpleasantness if a workman complained of wrongful dismissal or some such thing. Soldiers stopped us every ten or 12 miles on the road to town to 'inspect' our vehicle or our paperwork. Students became less and less prepared to obey 'foreign' leadership and threatened to report us to the local authority over almost anything that displeased them.

I had been nearly seven years at Nyankunde, helping to build the College, writing all the course material for classes, caring for 72 young men each year, as we trained them to take their place in the emerging health service in North-eastern Congo. Was it, perhaps, time to take a break? But how could I go home and leave the College without a director, the Government having legislated in 1966 that only a medical doctor with ten years experience in the Congo could be accepted as director of a nurses' training college? Much prayer was made, then my Mission agreed to my taking an extended furlough if someone could be found to replace me at Nyankunde. Just then two things happened! The Government changed its insistence on the ten years experience in the Congo clause, and two recently married doctors, Philip and Nancy Wood, applied to WEC to work at Nyankunde. God's amazing and perfect timing was displayed once again!

I left Congo at the end of September 1973, and came home to the UK to help care for my mother for as long as she needed me. We holidayed together in Cornwall, and we were given rooms on the ground floor of our WEC Headquarters, near London. Many were willing and able to help me to care for Mother in the way she deserved. She and I were both happy and rested. The Mission asked me to take a certain number of deputation meetings for them, particularly to challenge university Christian Unions and church youth groups with the enormous needs of two-thirds of our world to hear the gospel. And the Lord graciously blessed in these. At the same time, I wrote *He Gave Us a Valley*, the second part of my autobiography.

Then the invitation came from USA Mission Headquarters to go and take a series of meetings for them, all over the States and Canada. After prayerful consideration, and discussion with my mother, Mission leadership and my brother and sisters, it was agreed that I should go. In September 1975, I left for that long tour on the other side of the Atlantic. Nine days after my arrival in USA, my brother rang to tell me our mother was dying. She died on the tenth. I was not there. My heart felt bruised. Why had I left her? I had returned from Congo in order to be with my mother when she needed me. If God knew He was taking her home, why did He allow me to leave her just then? Somehow I was enabled to keep going through the tour. Then, early in February 1976, I discovered the lump. I had to come to terms with the fact that this might well signal the end of my missionary involvement. What next? At that moment, still in the USA, I received the annual report from the church in our part of the Congo, in which the leaders spelt out their need of a missionary to train their pastors, using French as the teaching medium. Previously, all teaching had been in Swahili or Bangala. Having written to the church (without explaining my reasoning) to offer to fulfil that need for a three-year term, I received no answer and the silence hurt. I felt unwanted, almost rejected. Years later, I heard that they *had* replied, and were surprised that I never wrote again to them. Their letter had gone astray.

Throughout eight years in training (1945-53) and the first twelve years in Congo (1953-65), I prayed to God that He would Give me this mountain!. Then seven years back in Congo at Nyankunde (1966-73) and two years at our headquarters caring for Mother (1973-75), He taught me that His work is done down in the valleys. 'He gave us a valley!', and now He was saying, 'Make this valley full of ditches!'

So I was to learn to go deeper down, to 'dig ditches', that were often unseen and unrecognised by others, but which God promised to fill with blessing for others. My first instinct was, 'OK, God, I'll dig you a Suez Canal!' but that was not what He asked for! My Lord wanted just daily, small obediences; He wanted me to do whatever needed to be done next, without needing to be thanked or recognised, without a pedestal or a halo. Some might even question my continuing right to be called a missionary as I had no particular sphere of service and no proper job description. Was I willing to be insecure, perhaps lonely, often away on travels with unknown people? Fortunately He did not fill out the picture too much at the start, or I might well have backed off! Had the Lord told Moses at the time of the vision of the burning bush all about the ten plagues and Pharaoh's obstinacy, and all about the grumblings and complainings of the Israelite people, possibly Moses would never have accepted God's call to go back to Egypt and deliver His people from the cruel hand of the Egyptian oppressor. No, God just told him at the outset that He was sending him to lead His people to the promised land. That was all. And that vision of the end of the story kept Moses going when the way seemed hard and long.

'You dig the ditch daily: I will fill it daily.'

So the next stage of my life's journey was established on that promise. That it might not be easy, that there might well be heartaches and deep problems on route, I was well aware. He did not promise me a bed of roses without thorns. But He did promise me that others would be blessed if I would obey and trust Him.

Chapter One

Digging a Ditch at the Missionary Training College

For more than twenty years of my life, my Mission had always been there, as it were, in the background of my thinking, in the person of my Field Leader in Congo, as well as all the staff at our London Headquarters. When I went home on furlough, my mother was always there. There had always been somewhere to go, whether in Congo or in the UK, a home where I was loved, respected, wanted, and where I had a sense of worth, a job to do and friends to support me in doing it. Now I suddenly felt adrift. What would God have me do?

Three months after my surgery in June 1976, I went to the WEC Home Staff Conference, asking if there was a specific job that I could do for them, a niche into which I could fit. There was considerable discussion, in public from the floor, and in private at the Executive Committee meeting. Then two suggestions were made to me. Firstly, would I write a book for the Mission, to supplement *The Four Pillars of WEC* that Norman Grubb had written more than ten years previously? The four pillars, as we called them, were four doctrines on which the Mission stood, in its ministry to the unreached peoples of the world. These pillars were sacrifice, faith, holiness and fellowship. Everyone knew that I had not been exactly enthusiastic about the booklet, *Four pillars of WEC*!

Sacrifice – all of us in WEC agreed that only by following the Lord Jesus Christ, who gave His very life that we might be saved, could we possibly be used by God to bring others to a knowledge of sins forgiven. But were we, the missionaries who served in WEC, actually living sacrificial lives? I, for one, wasn't. I always had sufficient to eat and to wear, a home, a car (of sorts!), and all needed possessions whilst in Congo. And I was always (almost always!) happy, surrounded by many faithful friends. I had to ask myself where the sacrifices in my life were?

Faith – we all agreed that only by the exercise of faith in the power of the preaching of the living Word of God could we reclaim lost people from the lure of the pleasures of this world and exhort them to put their trust in the Saviour. But were we actually exercising that faith? Were we seeing a local church built up in all the lands where we worked as a direct result of such faith? We trusted the Lord for material needs, and for our health, yes, but were we seeing people saved, being brought to the foot of the cross and rejoicing in the assurance of sins forgiven? For twenty years in Congo, I had spent almost all my time with Christians, training them to be evangelists, it is true, but not myself actually reaching out to the unsaved. Was I exercising faith to see a local church built up where God had placed me to work?

Holiness – again, we all agreed that our Lord Jesus Christ was altogether holy, 'without sin', found to be faultless even by Pilate. But could we, His followers, claim to be like Him? If we did not reflect Him in His spotless loveliness, how were others ever going to be drawn to Him, and rescued from a life of imperfections to a life of holiness? We knew we should be holy, but we also knew we were not. Even on the mission field there were squabbles and jealousies between us. Sometimes during my twenty years in Congo, I felt so conscious of being unholy, I wondered what right I had to be called a missionary at all!

And then **Fellowship** – we all agreed that none of us, working alone, could ever achieve what needed to be done in order to build a church in every remaining unreached people group. We knew we had to work in fellowship with each other, and with all others who had the same objective. But were we really seeking to behave like that? Had we not still our barriers, and pride in being ourselves? Were we not still unwilling to become merged with other groups, even though they had exactly the same goals as ourselves? And was our understanding of the concept of fellowship only one of methodology, and not actually a biblical principle? The fellowship that we know to exist between the three Persons of the Trinity – one of mutual submission and promotion – was that characteristic of all of us in WEC?

I just couldn't accept the booklet, *The Four Pillars,* as an actual, real expression of what we missionaries in the WEC family were like. And I had spoken out fairly bluntly and said so!

'Write us another book,' the WEC International Leader said to me, 'that will express these four basic principles in down-to-earth practical ways, by which we can measure ourselves!' That was one job they offered me.

Then secondly, the Conference suggested that I should go to our WEC Missionary Training College (MTC) in Glasgow for a year, to give me a chance to make a full recovery from all the various traumas I had gone through, before they considered a more permanent assignment. While at the College, it was suggested that I might help Chrissey Bachelor in the office, particularly with regard to the closing-down accounts. The College was due to close at the end of that academic year. Not that I knew a thing about official account-keeping! I had kept the accounts at Nebobongo for 12 years, and at Nyankunde Nurses' Training School for seven years, but those accounts would hardly have been accepted by an auditor! Using school exercise books, one side of each page headed 'IN' and the opposite page 'OUT', every transaction was meticulously entered. Each page was then carefully balanced, the money being kept in a row of empty Quaker Oats' tins, neatly labelled 'Hospital', 'Nurses',

'Wages', 'Truck', 'Leprosy work', etc. This was a somewhat 'Heath-Robinson' method, it is true, but it seemed adequate in the primitive area where we lived and worked. But now, in the UK?

So I travelled north to Glasgow, where I was warmly welcomed by staff and students, if a little hesitantly by some. How would I fit in? I was older than most of the staff, and all of the students. Would I want to boss them? That was when I first began to feel lonely. In all the years since I had become a Christian I had never experienced loneliness. I had always been so busy, always surrounded by so many companions, always on the stretch to accomplish the task in hand. Now, how would I fill my time? I didn't merely want them to find me a job to keep me occupied, if the job didn't really need doing. I needed to sense that I was needed.

Because I was part of the College staff, and they were short of lecturers, I was asked to take two courses in the MTC curriculum: a two-hour class each week with all the students, to survey World Missions, and a weekly class in the Book of Isaiah, with the small group of students who were sitting for an external Diploma in Biblical Knowledge and Christian Theology. I enjoyed the preparation needed for these lectures, but I still had a lot of time on my hands. I asked to attend Dave Burnett's lectures on Christian Theology to the Diploma students, Flora Gibson's lectures to the same group on John's Gospel, and Hywell Jones's lectures on Early Church History. This all included study work, the writing of essays, and eventually taking the Diploma exams with the students. I was quite excited by the challenge.

But still I had time. I was not used to that, and I found I didn't like it. I tried to help Chrissey in the office but felt pretty ignorant as I didn't understand 'double-entry system' and such like terms. And the fact that closing-down accounts of a non-profit-making organisation had to be presented in a particular way if they were to be accepted by the auditors made the task even more daunting. So I went to evening classes at the local technical college to study accountancy. That really stretched me and I enjoyed it.

However, underneath all these little bits and pieces of activity, there was a gnawing feeling that this was all somewhat superficial, a filling-in-of-time. Not that I was unwilling to be a gap-filler, if that was what the Lord wanted of me for that year, but in comparison to the previous 20 years, it all seemed unnecessary, a little unreal, and of no eternal value.

Before going to Glasgow, I had been invited by Dave Howard, Director of the Triennial Missionary Conference of the Inter-Varsity Christian Unions in the United States of America, to be one of the speakers at what is known as the Urbana Conference. The title that year, 1976, was 'Declare His Glory among the nations.' John Stott was to give the four Bible Studies on the Biblical basis of missions. Various challenges highlighting the needs in differing parts of the world were to be presented by well-known international speakers. Elisabeth Elliot was to direct the students' thinking on how to find the will of God for their lives, and then I was asked to speak on 'The cost of declaring God's glory to the nations.' Billy Graham would follow with a clear challenge to all those young people, offering them the opportunity to respond to God's voice. Then the last day would be given to thinking about 'How do we move forward? What do we do next, in order to follow through with our response to this challenge?'

To say I was very nervous, as I sought to prepare a twenty minute presentation, would be a gross understatement! I knew there would be 17,000 students there, as well as representatives from over 100 missionary agencies, some of the best known missionary speakers from all over the world, Bible College and Missionary Training College faculties and a host of such like people. And I was deeply conscious of not being in the same league. I was not an experienced public speaker, nor a missiologist. Why had I accepted Dave's invitation? I asked myself. God reminded me that I accepted because I believed that this was God's will for me at that time. If it was God's will, why was I so terrified? Could I not trust God to give me the word He wanted me to share with those young people?

Then, during the October half-term weekend at the College, I was invited to Birmingham, to speak at Shirley Baptist Church. On the Saturday evening, they asked me to speak on 'Why does a God of love allow such suffering?' This referred mainly to all that our group of missionaries, as well as the Congolese Christians, went through in the Congo civil war in the 1960s. I shared as fully and openly as I could, including the fact that anything that we suffered was as nothing compared to what our Lord Jesus Christ suffered for us, and how He helped us all to see suffering as a *privilege* – something we shared with Him, what the Bible calls 'the fellowship of sharing in His sufferings'. In fact, God reminded me of how, just a quarter of an hour after I first came to realise, as a 19-year-old, the wonder of the fact that Christ Jesus died for my sins, a wise and godly man gave me the verse: '*I want to know Christ and the power of his resurrection and the fellowship of sharing in his sufferings, becoming like him in his death, and so, somehow, to attain to the resurrection from the dead*' (Phil. 3:10, 11), he had prayed for me, 'Perhaps one day God will give you the privilege of sharing in the fellowship of His suffering'. So my whole Christian life started with the assurance that to suffer for the cause of Christ was to be considered as a privilege, nor merely as the price of service. The family at Shirley Baptist Church took me up on the thought of 'privilege rather than price,' and, on the Sunday evening, I was asked to speak on this. As I prepared for that meeting, the Lord really spoke to my own heart.

God reminded me that my call to missionary service, in what was then the Belgian Congo, had been through Isaiah 58:1-12, which ends with the sentence '*You will be called the Repairer of Broken Walls.*' The word used in the Swahili for 'the Repairer' is really 'a gap-filler', the same word as is used in Ezekiel 22:30

'*I looked for a man among them who would build up the wall and stand before Me in the gap .. but I found none.*' God's call to me was to be a gap-filler. Was I not now willing to fulfil that calling or did I want something bigger and better? Did I want a job description that others could read and understand, or was I willing to be in the background and do what needed doing, even if never thanked? And I suddenly saw this as *privilege*, not price! So many of the things that we think of as price in a missionary's life (giving up of home, culture, language, rat-race, salary, being married and having one's own family, pension, whatever) is truly privilege. It is the amazing privilege of being identified with our Lord Jesus, who had nowhere to lay His head, and had to borrow a donkey, a penny and a tomb.

After the evening service, several members of the congregation came to thank me for being God's mouthpiece to them, to rebuke them for grumbling at the 'price' to be paid, and to urge them to rejoice at the 'privilege' of sharing with Him. And my heart was filled with joy! How good of God to have graciously spoken *through* me to the blessing of others, when He was busy trying to speak *to* me at the very same time! Then the Lord clearly told me that this was the theme I was to use at Urbana: the cost is only another way of saying the price – and the price is actually the privilege!

I went back to College and sought to put this into practice, to see each small task as a privilege, no matter what others thought. At least with my lips I could state that these were privilege rather than price, but I knew my heart wasn't really in the exercise. I had no real joy in the life I was living. To a degree I was submissive to the leadership, in that I fulfilled each duty with meticulous care and no longer grumbled. But what about the Scripture that says: 'I delight to do Thy will, O my God!' (Ps.40:8 KJV)? In my innermost being, I was not rejoicing, let alone delighting. Instead I was daily hankering for the past. I longed to go back to Congo, to take up my responsibilities again at either Nebobongo or Nyankunde, to be stretched and fulfilled, to be happy and satisfied. I was feeling increasingly useless in my new role.

This hankering for the past led to doubting the present. Was I still listening to *God*'s voice, and only His voice, to direct me, or was I now dependent on the voice of the Mission? Was I staying at home as a gap-filler because *God* wanted to give me a new direction, or because I was afraid of the soldiers, harassment, nervous tensions, and everything that welled up in my mind when I seriously thought of going back to Congo? Then there was that unanswered letter in which I had offered to go back despite my fears. The lack of an answer from the African Church in Congo made me feel that they were not ready to welcome me back. That hurt. It led to a sense of rejection. To be honest, I knew I had not always been popular with my missionary colleagues as I had often been too outspoken. And I knew that others felt I had been too keen to trust, and hand over leadership to, National Christians. But I thought I was acceptable to the African Church. Did they really not want me back?

Over and over again, the word spoke to me about living one day at a time. I was so aware of all the present tense activities of God, whose Name is 'I am'. Had He not promised Paul: 'My grace *is* sufficient for you, for my power *is* made perfect in weakness'? Flora brought this out when she was teaching us from the 'I am' statements of the Lord Jesus Christ in John's Gospel. 'I *am* the Bread of Life' 'I *am* the Good Shepherd'. These are in the present tense to remind us that God is all of the great 'I am' statements right now, to meet our needs right now, whatever they are. They are present day promises to equip us for the present day. I had to learn that God was all I needed to enable me to throw myself wholeheartedly and unreservedly into my present commitments, without comparing them with past achievements or possible future activities.

God enabled me, at least at that time, to take hold of this challenge and to throw myself into all the daily tasks to which I was assigned with renewed energy *and joy*. I actually became quite proficient in account-keeping, which was specially useful as Chrissey was having a bad time with arthritis. Flora slipped a disc in her back and I was available to help her. In fact, I spent a lot of time in her room, taking her meals, doing what I could to help her to rest, as well as studying for the upcoming end-of-year exams. Lecture preparation with the students was really rewarding and helped me feel back in my stride. God graciously blessed as I took my eyes off myself and what I wanted or felt, and fixed my eyes back on Jesus and all He had done for me.

In between all the other activities I was trying to begin jotting down thoughts towards the book I had been invited to write, starting with the first pillar – sacrifice. Slowly, the general outline of what I believed God wanted me to write began to take shape. I realised that each 'pillar' was likely to turn into a small booklet on its own rather than be a chapter in a larger book. The ministry at Shirley Baptist Church in November of that year and then Urbana in December, especially the thoughts God put into my heart regarding 'Price or Privilege?' (or 'the Cost of Declaring His Glory') became my starting-off point – how God needs to whittle each one of us, like forming an arrow from a rough branch by removing the flowers and leaves, the side branches and thorns, even the bark itself, everything that would render the arrow less than useful – so that He can use us as He choses. We so easily see the whittling process as the *price* we have to pay to become what the Lord God plans for us, but in actual fact, it will eventually be seen as the only means by which we can enjoy the full *privilege* that He longs to give us.

That was how the Lord enabled me to present His truth at Urbana during the Christmas holiday. It was a shattering experience, standing there before that mass of students, in the huge assembly hall of the University of Illinois. John Stott encouraged me by saying, 'Don't look at 17,000 faces, just look at someone in the front row. All the rest are repetitions!' His words of wisdom helped me through. After I spoke there, using a huge visual aid that our WEC Canadian Headquarters made for me, I looked forward very much to hearing Dr Billy Graham speak. Every time he had been to the UK since his first mission in 1953, I had been unable to hear him as I was in Congo. So that evening I managed to secure a front-row seat among those reserved for speakers and seminar leaders, and sat with pen and paper, ready to listen intently to his message to those students, hoping to learn from him how one could present a meaningful challenge for world missions to the student world. Billy Graham stood – he was such a humble and unassuming man and I could see him clearly. Then, overwhelmed by the relief that my own message was now over, I fell asleep and never heard a word! On my way home after the conference, I took my visual aid with me – a six-foot long artificial branch of forsythia, with huge green leaves and bright yellow flowers made of polystyrene, and enclosing a gigantic arrow, fitted with a pointed end that showed up on X-rays as a potential weapon. At each customs checkpoint I had to explain the reason for carrying such a thing with me!

The College year back in Glasgow was drawing to a close. The final accounts were presented and accepted by the auditors. Thank You, Lord! The group of students who sat the Diploma examination all passed, some with distinction. Thank You, Lord! Several of the students, at the end of term, testified to having heard the Lord's voice clearly directing them to their future spheres of service through the World Mission Survey lectures. Thank You, Lord! Chapter One of the booklet on sacrifice had taken shape, and Flora, who read it for me, was excited by it. Thank You, Lord! And even as I write this page, many years later, I have just received an e-mail from someone who wants to meet me, an assistant professor at a university in USA, who says that she first heard me at Urbana in 1976, at which time she was deeply blessed by what God gave me to say. How utterly amazing. Thank You, Lord!

Were these all 'ditches' successfully dug and then graciously filled by the Lord? If so, what was the next step to be? As I looked back and praised God for all His wonderful undertaking for me, I could see that my twenty years of service in Congo might have been essential training for the present sphere of service. So much that occurred during the nine-month tour of meetings in the USA the previous year, and then at the College, could not really have impacted others if I had not been through the training school of the previous twenty years in Congo. That was fairly easy to say, but the inference was not so easy to accept. Was the present preparing me for the next tomorrow? And if so, what was it to be?

Dave and Anne Burnett would have loved me to go with them to the London Headquarters of our Mission, where they believed God would have them start a new Missionary Orientation Course (MOC), to serve all evangelical missions in the preparation of their candidates. But I just did not feel any rise in my spirit towards this. I was willing to go, should WEC feel this was the right place for me, but I was not excited by the thought of such an assignment. Actually, I helped the Burnetts pack up the College: library books, missiological records, various teaching aids and materials, as well as desks and chairs, dining room furniture and equipment, bedroom furnishings – everything moveable! – into hired vans, which Dave and others drove south to our Mission Headquarters. We talked and prayed about his vision for the future, and his definite need of others to come alongside him to put it all into practice. But still my heart did not rise to the challenge.

Should I take some further training in order to be of more use to Dave, or to some other similar project in WEC? Or was I to continue in a speaking ministry for them, as a roving deputation worker on full-time home assignment? I felt so insecure in this latter role. I did not feel that I was adept at relating to other people. I was not what people called a natural communicator, however much my heart beat for missions.

During the summer holiday, I went as a leader to a Girl Crusaders' Union (GCU) 'camp' in Scotland. They had hired the Aberlour Boys' Prep School for two weeks, where sixty girls (10 to 17 year olds) from all over the UK were brought together, with some twelve leaders (mature Christian women, appointed to leadership in one of the many weekly Bible Classes in Scotland, England, Wales and Ireland), to enjoy a first-rate holiday with games, outings and activities in a Christian environment, with daily prayer times and Bible studies. I was an Assistant Leader with GCU before I first went to Congo, and was invited back into the ranks to help in the task of 'handing on the baton' to the next generation. It was a marvellous camp, and certainly reassured me that one of the special ministries God had entrusted to me over many years was teaching His Word and challenging young people to a wholehearted devotion to Jesus Christ and obedience to that Word.

How was this going to help me find direction for the next phase of my life's journey? All I wanted was to please God. I did not want to please myself, nor merely fill in time. But how was I to be sure what I should be doing? Before my mother's death, she and I thought about the possibility of my teaching in one of the UK's Bible Colleges, and certainly my joy at being in the teaching ministry, both at the Missionary Training College throughout the year, and again at the GCU Camp in the summer, made me think again about this idea. One such college had actually invited me for an interview, with the suggestion that I join the staff for a year. That would have given me a settled place, a clear 'job description' and security. Was that what the Lord wanted?

'Please, God,' I prayed earnestly, 'I need a clear word from Yourself.'

And the Holy Spirit reminded me that He had spoken clearly, just the previous year, 'Make this valley full of ditches', and He indicated that the task was not yet completed. So I waited to see the next step.

Chapter Two

~~~~~~

Digging a Ditch
on the Deputation Trail

I spent a lovely two weeks after the GCU Camp at Aberlour,
with my friend Patricia and her mother, at a country-house
hotel in Morayshire. The weather was perfect. We visited many
of the surrounding beauty spots in northeast Scotland, including
looking down on Balmoral Castle. We walked on hillsides and on
beaches. We watched salmon jumping in the Dee and had time
to reflect, refresh and renew for the upcoming year. Patricia and
I met each other through the GCU summer camp at Aberlour
the previous year. With her mother, she had offered me to share
their home, near Belfast in Northern Ireland, whenever I needed
a base from which to work. So now, on holiday together, we
prayed about what God would have me do in the coming year,
but had no specific guidance.

At the end of August, I had been invited to take part in the
Bangor Missionary Convention in Northern Ireland. On the
Thursday evening, speaking to a packed congregation on the
privilege of being one of God's ambassadors (2 Cor. 5:17–21),
I was suddenly deeply conscious of His overruling power and
presence. At an after-meeting that same evening, some 200 young
people were prepared and willing to be challenged about how
they could be involved. I remember stripping a lovely rose to
create an arrow (the same illustration as I had used at the Urbana

Student Missionary Conference in USA the previous winter, but in miniature!) and an intense, almost audible, silence settled over them.

I pulled the flowers and leaves off the rose. It looked like wanton destruction, but in the other hand I held up an arrow. There was nothing wrong with the flowers and leaves. In fact, they were essential to the life of the rose. Without them the rose could not breathe, feed or reproduce. But they would be a hindrance to the functioning of an arrow if left on the branch. Would we allow God to strip us, even of good things in our lives if, by doing so, He could make us into instruments more useable in His service? If He asked us to forego the right to well paid jobs and future security, to marriage, having a family and our own home, to advancement in our professions, or to popularity or general success, could we say 'Yes' to the Lord and trust Him to mould us into the patterns He has planned for us?

I cut off thorns and side branches. There was nothing wrong with these for the rose, but they certainly wouldn't help the balance of the arrow. Would we allow God to strip off our 'rights': our right to order our own lives, to decide our life's partner, to choose our jobs and places of work, or our right to be considered, to have our opinions asked when decisions were made that affected our own lives, or even our right to own and possess the basic necessities of decent living conditions? Were we willing to '*throw off everything that hinders and the sin that so easily entangles*': the sins of impatience, a critical spirit, the need to justify ourselves and our every action, the sin of being unwilling to be falsely accused and misunderstood? Could we hand all this over to the Lord and trust Him entirely with complete control of our lives? I spoke to myself as well as to the others present.

But the bare stem I held in my hand – devoid of flowers and leaves, stripped of thorns and side branches – was still recognisable as the branch of a rose. I took a knife and whittled away the bark. Had even the bark to go? The bark gave the rose its individuality; it made it recognisable for what it was. The bark protected it from rain and sun. But now the shaft left in my hand, polished and smooth, could be seen to be useable as an arrow. Would we allow God the right to invade our innermost beings, to strip us naked of ourselves, so that others looking at us would see only Jesus? Were we willing to give up our right to be ourselves in order to be wholly identified with Him, and so available to Him for whatever He wants and plans for our lives?

We stayed late that evening, talking and praying with individuals ... and I simply knew that God was saying to me, 'This is the work I want to do through you. The fact that you do not consider yourself to be a communicator is good; you will trust Me and leave Me to do My own work. The fact that you are uncomfortable in this ministry, feeling that you are not trained for it or particularly good at it, is partly why I have chosen you. You will always know that any blessing that results will not be to your glory, but will be wholly Mine.'

I had most of September to think that over and to pray about it, until I came to a somewhat reluctant agreement that I would do what God was asking me to do. Part of my reluctance lay in the fact that I was still hankering after a return to Congo. Was I willing to simply lay that at God's feet? Pat and I received a copy of *Parables of the Cross*, one of Lilias Trotter's books, for a Christmas present that year. I had long loved Trotter's books, but all my copies were destroyed in Congo in the rebellion of 1964. One of the paragraphs in *Parables of the Cross* is headed 'Death to Lawful Things is the Way Out into a Life of Surrender.'

There is a painting of three buttercups, one just a bud beginning to open, a second is half open, and the third and central one is fully open, with the sepals folded right back. 'Look at this buttercup,' wrote Lilias, 'as it begins to learn its new lesson. The little hands of the calyx clasp tightly in the bud, round the beautiful petals. In the young flower their grasp grows more elastic – loosening somewhat in the daytime, but keeping the power of contracting, able to close in again during a rainstorm or when night comes on. But see the central flower, which has reached its maturity. The calyx hands have unclasped utterly now – they have folded themselves back, past all power of closing again upon the petals, leaving the golden crown free to float away when God's time comes.'

Had I learned the buttercup's lesson yet? Would I take my hands, once and for all time, off every part of my life and leave God completely free to do with me and through me whatever He chose? Or was I still in the phase of partial relaxing of my grasp, with power to take things back again when the going got tough? I wanted to say 'Yes!' to God, with complete abandonment, with nothing held back. And yet, I so easily took back and took hold again when I felt insecure or fearful.

I was invited by our WEC Scottish Representative, Roy Spraggett, to go to Scotland for a tour of meetings with him, quickly followed by a week of meetings across the north of England, and then down to Bristol and South Wales for two weeks. I crossed over to Scotland by ferry, with my small car, and headed out into the unknown with a vengeance! Roy was a wonderful and understanding companion and he quickly realised my sense of insecurity. As we drove to a meeting, he would quietly quiz me about the topic on which I was going to speak. If I hesitated, uncertain between two different approaches, he would draw off the road into a parking area and suggest we prayed together. After committing the next meeting to the Lord, he often suggested what he felt might be the best way to present the challenge of missions to that particular group. Then we would think it through together until I sensed a quietness in my spirit, that this was truly the Lord's way. The meetings were enormously varied: a church youth group, a children's talk in the morning service, a women's coffee morning and a valedictory service for one of our Scottish missionaries going out to Chad. I was amazed at how the Lord was able to speak through us to each different age group, and to people of completely differing backgrounds.

From Scotland to the north of England, from Southport in the west to Doncaster in the east, we travelled and we spoke. Again, there was the continual stretch of being willing for any situation at a moment's notice, including speaking at a Communion service on the Sunday, and a women's evangelistic outreach meeting on the Tuesday, ten minutes at a School Assembly – where the children had never heard of WEC – followed by forty minutes at a WEC regional rally, where everyone was already deeply involved in missions! Then I drove south to Bristol, and across into South Wales from Newport to Swansea, where my programme included a radio interview, meetings in a Bible college and two sessions in a huge comprehensive school. It was wonderful to share in a packed midweek meeting in Heath Church, Cardiff, and another in Mount Pleasant Baptist Church, Swansea.

Throughout that month, I seemed always to be packing my suitcase and moving on. I slept in a different bed almost every night, and met with new people every day. Hundreds of people would gladly have been my friends, but there was no time to develop friendships. I found that each day I had to try to forget yesterday's people, in order to relate to those of today. The pace was fairly unrelenting. In between meetings, if there was ever a spare minute, letters had to be written to thank very kindly and generous families for their hospitality. And, if there was yet another gap in the programme, I tried to complete the manuscript of *Living Sacrifice*, the first of the series to present WEC's four pillars.

It really was all a little breathtaking. I managed four days at my new 'home' with Pat and her mother, on the outskirts of Belfast, but even these days included four meetings! Then I was off to Dublin for a packed week, then back to thirty-six meetings in the following four weeks. Thank God for a quiet Christmas at home, to look back over those three months, and try to evaluate and to look forward, and try not to plan! All I knew for certain was that God had undertaken in an amazing way. I was quite certain that I could never, never have taken all those meetings in my own strength. But I did begin to wonder if God really meant me to keep up such a pace. Then a few letters began to come telling of this one and that one who had been blessed or challenged at the meetings. So I had dug another ditch and, unknown to me, unseen and unheard, God graciously filled it with life-giving water.

Others wrote, and I sensed an underlying urgency as though the writer wanted to say something or ask me something, but was hesitating – trying me out, perhaps, as to whether they could trust me or not. My replies, thanking writers for their letters and offering friendship, were always written by hand lest type-written letters – this was before the days of computers or emails – would make people suspect there was a secretary involved, and therefore no absolute privacy and confidentiality. Then a second letter often followed in which the writer unburdened her heart, and sought counsel and spiritual help. Such correspondence began to take more and more of my time, but seemed to be very definitely part of God's planned 'ditches' for me.

Early in January, I was on the south coast of England for a weekend of meetings. On the Wednesday that followed, I drove 400 miles north to Durham for an evening meeting at the university. It started to snow, and the journey was not an easy one. I was running short on petrol by the time I reached the university car park, and I asked the Lord that, should the secretary of the meeting give me a gift, that it should please be in cash and not a cheque, as a cheque wouldn't buy me petrol. At the end of the evening, I *was* handed an envelope – but it contained a book-token! *That* wouldn't buy petrol either. Driving south the next day, I used every penny I had to put petrol in the car, and prayed that God would somehow get me to London! The next evening, I stayed with Roger Carswell and his family in Garforth, and spoke to over 300 working folk in a small crowded hall. At the end of the evening they emptied the offering box into my handbag. What a heavy weight of coins! Bless their hearts; they more than covered all my needs from Worthing to Durham, and back again! I was humbled and amazed. In my quick judgement

– looking at the outward appearance and not the heart – the Garforth group had not appeared to be in a position to supply my needs. But God knew otherwise. This was a lesson I was to learn many times in the ensuing years. While I was to ask God to supply my needs, I was not to work out how He would supply them. I didn't have to tell God His own job, and He never let me down. There was always what was needed, just at the time it was needed.

Back again in the south for a week of meetings, I became sick with 'flu. Leaving the home where I was staying on the south coast to drive to Hildenborough Hall, I met heavy snow, traffic diversions, hold-ups as well as accidents. And all the way I felt more and more unwell. I tried to telephone the people who were expecting me in Sevenoaks, to say it was very unlikely I would get there by 7 p.m. ready for an evening meeting. But the telephone lines were down. Struggling on, I managed about three miles in half an hour. Should I turn back to the south? I asked myself. That is what I saw others doing. But I knew that the people where I had stayed the previous night had other guests coming that day, and it would be very inconvenient for them to have me, especially as I was becoming increasingly unwell. I was upset, and not sure what I ought to do. Sticking at it, I crawled up a long winding icy hill – slithering and skithering – when suddenly there was no more snow. The sun came out and there were no more cars, as most people had turned back! I managed to reach my host's home by 8 p.m., very weary, pretty sick, and full of apologies for being so late, only to hear that they had cancelled the meeting because of the weather. I was beginning to learn that God amazingly undertakes in all sorts of situations and I don't need to panic. I had all the tender loving care I needed in that home for the next three days, until I was really fit enough to move on to my next engagement. How good God was to me!

However, that attack of 'flu left me with quite severe laryngitis, and no voice. I drove on to Kings Lynn where I was to speak in the large and lovely Anglican church in the morning and to an after-church rally in the evening. They had one of the most sophisticated sound amplification systems I had ever spoken into, one that multiplied my faint whisper until it filled the whole church! Once again, God graciously turned a difficult moment into one of praise to Him.

From there I went to a whole week of meetings in Oxford University, and then home to Belfast for four weeks to prepare for a month of meetings spanning the United States. There were over forty public engagements booked, and we had to cover over 2,000 miles by car. The Easter weekend services were very uplifting and the six Bible colleges were all very challenging. But I remember especially one evening when I met with some 400 university students in the Twin City Bible Church, in Urbana. I had been asked to speak to the subject 'The Cost of being a missionary', probably by a student who had heard me speak to the subject at the Urbana Conference the previous year.

As I entered the lecture theatre and made my way down to the front, I noticed two girls sitting together, about five rows from the front on my left. One of them seemed much too young to be a student, and there was something strange about the way she looked at me. I wondered if she was blind, appearing to look in my direction, but not actually seeing me. I gave my talk, basing my thoughts on the four letters, C – O – S – T, and illustrating, as I had done in Bangor, by stripping a rose to make an arrow. Part way through my presentation, I sensed the Lord 'nudging' me to tell, in a little more detail than usual, what I had suffered on the night of October 28th 1964, when the guerrilla soldiers captured me. I shared how they struck me over and over again with the butt end of their guns, how I fell and they kicked me, breaking two or three of my back teeth, how they dragged me to my feet and forced me back to the veranda of my home and how the brutal leader raped me. I passed over this as quickly as I could, but shared with those students how God spoke to me in my distress, asking me to '*thank* Him for trusting me with such an experience, even if He never told me why.'

At the close of the meeting, I went up to the back of the hall to speak to students as they left. Then I returned to the front to collect my Bible and notes, and there were the two girls waiting to speak to me. The older one asked me if I had time to speak with her younger sister. 'She was raped six weeks ago, and since then no-one has been able to help her. She will not speak to any of us: her family, our doctor, our minister at church, no-one.' I turned to the younger girl and looked straight at her. She stood up, and slowly began to come towards me. Then, suddenly, she ran at me, threw her arms round my neck and burst into tears. We sat down together, and slowly she unloaded, sharing all that had been bottling up inside her for the six weeks since the horrifying incident. She ended by saying, 'No-one told me that I could **thank** the Lord for trusting me with this!' We prayed together, and thanked Him for His love and grace towards us, for all He has done for us, and then for trusting us. When God could have saved us from the horror, He actually trusted us to go through the ordeal *with Him*, so that He could use the experience later to help others. We cried together, hugged each other then I said goodnight to the two of them.

Later that evening, I thanked God again for letting me know, at least in some small measure, the why of that long-ago night in the Congo. God didn't have to show me why He allowed the ordeal; I had accepted it all from His hands unquestioningly. But now I knew that at least one young girl had been helped to come to terms with the shock, *because* I was enabled to share from my own experience. Thank You, God! The fact that the Lord 'nudged' me to share that particular incident, that particular night, when it was not part of my prepared notes, also amazed me at His great goodness. If only we would trust Him utterly to overrule in every situation.

There followed two months at home – a welcome break, with only a few local meetings. During that time I worked hard, trying to complete the manuscript for *Living Sacrifice*. I had sent the rough draft to our WEC International Office for their critical evaluation, and was now working on the grammar and 'polishing' the presentation. The way in which people reacted at so many of the meetings, both in the UK and also in the USA, helped me to word some things differently, or led me to leave illustrations out or develop others. The book began with a realisation of the great sacrifice made by our Lord Jesus Christ, the very Son of God, when He died on the cruel Cross of Calvary, for *my* sins. There is no sacrifice that I can ever make that can ever come near to His sacrifice. In fact, every effort on my part to respond to His great love to me, to thank Him for all He has achieved by His death that I might know forgiveness of sin, can only be seen as *privilege*. That my Saviour should not only save me from the guilt and penalty of my sins, but that He should then invite me to be His co-labourer, to work with Him and for Him in His worldwide vineyard, that others might come to a knowledge of salvation – that is just tremendous privilege!

How can we show God that we love Him? How can we express our thanks to Him for all He has done for us at Calvary? '*Whoever has my commandments and obeys them, he is the one who loves me*' (John 14:21). And what are His commandments that I should seek to obey? '*Love the Lord your God with all your heart and with all your soul and with all your mind and with all your strength,*' and '*Love your neighbour as yourself*' (Mark 12:29-31). I set out in the book to explore whether, of my 20 years of missionary service in Congo, I could conceivably testify that I *had* loved my Lord with *all* my heart, mind, soul and strength. I was horrified to realise how often I failed to do this, and recognising the failures really helped me to see what should have been done on many, many occasions.

In the introductory chapter of *Living Sacrifice*, I shared a story of how our village of Nebobongo had been invaded by thousands of weaver birds that destroyed our palm trees, stripping the fronds to make their nests. We challenged the primary school children, telling them that for every dead weaver bird brought to us we would pay them a penny. The children loved it! They stripped our bright yellow acacia trees to make arrows, and then set about killing birds by the dozens! But to destroy the pest, they had also destroyed the beauty of our acacia trees. Yet at the same time, they had saved our palms and their maturing nuts that provided our essential oil for food. Was the 'gain' worth the cost? From there the book developed, seeking to underline the essential truth that any apparent cost on our part is more than compensated by the enormous privilege our Lord gives us as we serve Him and put Him wholly first in our lives.

Having sent the manuscript to our WEC International Leadership for their criticisms, I waited a little fearfully. Was this the sort of book they wanted me to write? Would they understand what I was trying to say? Then I received a shattering invitation to attend the six-yearly conference of all our WEC Mission leaders from all home bases and from all fields worldwide AND to give one of the presentations on the 'Four Pillars' at a morning devotional session. I was deeply humbled. I am not a leader in our Mission and I was almost overwhelmed at the thought of being at their conference. When I arrived at Kilcreggan House in the West of Scotland, where we were all to meet for three whole weeks, I sought out any job I could do to be helpful: assisting the official Conference Secretary in taking notes, making cups of tea, helping in the kitchen, preparing vegetables and washing up, helping some of our national brothers from other lands to find their way around, anything that I could do to help me justify my presence among them all! In between times, I went over and over the notes I had prepared for my presentation on 'Sacrifice'.

The day before the meeting, I asked the head gardener for a rose – or any suitable branch – with which to illustrate my talk. I explained to him that my visual aid needed flowers, leaves, thorns, side branches and bark. Arriving in the hall early the next morning, I saw in front of the podium, a HUGE floral display of rhododendron. It was truly magnificent, covered with glorious blossoms and glossy leaves. But as I looked at it in awe, I realised that I could not possibly break off a branch in the

middle of my talk. It was far too massive. So I set to, sawed
a branch off, and then stuck it back on with adhesive tape. When
I eventually cut it off during my talk, with a small penknife, it
looked comparatively easy! As I stood there, with the branch in
my hand, and almost nonchalantly started to pull off the flowers
and then strip off the leaves, there was an audible gasp of horror
– especially from the men!

'What are you doing? That is wanton destruction of a thing of
great beauty!' Then a deep silence settled over the whole group as
they began to see the relevance of the visual aid to the message.
Were we, as a Mission, prepared for, and willing to accept, the
deliberate laying aside of beauty in our plans and programs, in our
abilities and even our visions, if God showed us this would lead
to the fulfilment of His plan and purposes? There were tears shed.
There were many inner battles fought, and yet throughout that
day God wrought a deep new inner peace in many hearts as we
allowed Him to lead us to the point of saying, 'Yes, Lord, whatever
it costs!'

During that time of conference, we heard news of the fearful
massacre of thirteen missionaries and their children, including
a baby, in Zimbabwe, and we all prayed, 'Lord, if that had been
me, could I have said "Yes" to You?' In the weeks that followed,
we heard something of the blessing amongst the national children
in the school where those missionaries had been teaching. We
saw that God had asked them for the ultimate sacrifice that He
might complete His work in the hearts of some of the older boys
and girls there. Humanly, one was tempted to ask, 'Is there always
a price to pay for blessing? Has God the right to demand that
of those missionaries and of their families back home?' But the
Spirit pressed us to look through the immediate to the ultimate.
Those missionaries were all now in glory; their work was complete.
And some of our group, in the prayer time that followed the
announcement of this news, voiced all our thoughts. 'Dear Lord,
help us to see that the stripping of the rose results in the formation
of the arrow as an instrument in Your hands to perfect Your will.'

At the close of the Mission's Conference, I had a few further meetings, then most of September was spent back at home. That allowed me time for prayer and refreshment, and for preparing three months of meetings that had been lined up, meetings that would keep me travelling and speaking until the following Christmas.

Chapter Three

Digging Ditches in Preparing Messages and Building up Relationships

By the autumn of 1978, the preparation of the manuscript of *Living Sacrifice* was completed, ready for submission to the publishers. Meetings went on, much as previously, including ten days at Aberlour at a GCU camp for schoolgirls, and a very welcome summer holiday. With nearly 80 public meetings booked for the three months up to Christmas, it was essential to take time for prayerful consideration of how I could present the missionary challenge in different ways. Each day of my summer break I sought to pray through the meetings of each day of the upcoming tour. But I didn't always know ahead of time what any day would bring forth. Sometimes I arrived at a meeting expecting teenagers, to find the children were all primary school age, or a meeting I thought was for women turned out to be a mixed congregation.

The first time this happened, in 1975 in America, it taught me a tremendous lesson about trusting the Lord for last minute guidance. I arrived at a church one Sunday morning at 10 a.m. expecting to give a short twenty minute devotional message to the whole congregation. The pastor met me, and explained that the first hour, from 10 a.m. to 11a.m. was Sunday School, and asked if I would be willing to speak to the senior group? I knew I was expected to say 'Yes', but my mind raced, trying to think which of my prepared messages would be suitable. I flicked through my file, and picked out the notes on a message for senior teenagers, with three African stories to illustrate the dangers of sex, drink and drugs.

I was ushered into a room for the Senior Sunday School class to find myself surrounded by some thirty Senior Citizens, all white haired and very welcoming! I nearly died. I had not understood the American use of the term 'Sunday School'. My choice of message, to put it mildly, seemed somewhat unsuitable. But God graciously came to my rescue. The lady leading the meeting asked them all if anyone had any special requests for prayer. When no-one responded, she handed the meeting over to me, and I said, 'Yes, I have a request for your prayers, please.' Then I shared with them how, that very week, my dear mother had died. As I spoke, I broke down and cried, and all 30 of those men and women cried with me. Then I shared with them my mother's testimony, and all she had meant to me. Later, when we went to the main sanctuary, I knew that scattered among the large congregation there were thirty dear men and women praying for me in a special and understanding way.

On another occasion, three of us left our WEC Headquarters in Philadelphia at about 5 a.m. on a cold and snowy morning, to drive to a Women's Breakfast on the East Coast. Based on some experience in the UK, I expected the women attending the meeting to be on their way to work, and so prepared a message based on the testimony of one of my African friends, Damaris, a lovely gentle person, who radiated the love of Jesus in all her work as a midwife at the Nebobongo maternity unit. Damaris really lived a Christ-like life, as described in 1 Corinthians 13, a life of practical, meaningful love. When we eventually arrived and entered the golf-club, we found ourselves surrounded by a very – what shall I say? – elite and sophisticated group of some 200 ladies. Seated at the top table, and looking round, I felt that my story of a simple African working woman just wasn't right. I surreptitiously opened my file and started looking through it for more suitable notes for this particular group. I pulled one such out, but still wasn't convinced that it was right. I slipped it back into the file, and looked for another one. My two WEC companions were watching me from their table in the hall, and they began praying that the Lord would give me His peace as they realised my obvious confusion. Then a lady was asked to sing a solo, and she sang – most beautifully and with deep conviction and meaning – a setting of the thirteenth chapter of Paul's first letter to the Corinthians!

I took out the notes I had prayerfully prepared before coming to the meeting, asked the Lord to forgive me for hesitating, and gave the simple talk that He originally prompted me to give. And, of course, it was just right for that group of ladies. When would I learn to trust the Lord, and His leading, rather than my own feelings? And how gracious of Him to give me that clear confirmation at the critical moment!

Another similar sort of lesson had to do with numbers, because I had to learn not to play the numbers game. I had a phone call once, inviting me to a large city in USA, to a church weekend conference where I would have the opportunity (as I thought the voice said) of speaking to 12,000 teenagers. I actually had another meeting booked for that same weekend, a Mothers' Union in a local church, where I could expect some 30 or so to attend. I managed to rearrange the timetable, and flew to the States for the weekend of meetings in Detroit, where I met with around 1,200 people, some of whom were teenagers, and where, by and large, they were not prepared for the challenge I felt I should give. It was a difficult and rather unhappy time, with no apparent response.

I had fallen for the temptation of believing that 12,000 teenagers were more important than thirty women. In fact, the voice on the phone had probably said twelve hundred, and I had misheard and misinterpreted, and so jumped to a wrong conclusion. But God spoke to me clearly, following that experience, telling me that HE was in charge, and that booked meetings were not to be changed for later invitations. He could control the timing of invitations, and in His eyes every single person was as important as any other. Number counting was not to be taken into account. I'm not sure that I have fully learned the lesson yet, but I do understand the principle involved.

One of the meetings I was invited to taught me a clear lesson in preparing material to present to others. The headmistress of a school for over 200 severely physically handicapped children in South-east Belfast, invited me to speak at a morning assembly to all the children and maybe almost as many staff. 'Please bring them a missionary challenge!' My mind was shocked. How does one present a *missionary* challenge to young people, some unable to control hands or feet, some tied to beds for their own protection, many in wheelchairs?

Then a small local event occurred. Belfast was struck by a series of electricity power cuts. Every household brought out, or went to the stores to buy, hurricane lanterns, oil and matches, in order to cope with the emergency. Our lantern was pretty ancient – battered, cracked paint, lost handle – but it did not leak. I polished up its glass, filled it with oil, and brought it into service. Our next-door neighbours bought themselves a shiny new lantern. Seeing it gave me an idea, and I asked them if I could borrow it on the day that I was to go to the school. Both lanterns were cleaned, filled with oil, but only one glass was polished; the other was painted with shoe-black!

At the school, with the help of a match, I lit the first lantern. It shone brightly. The light went in from outside, was fed by the oil, and shone out unhindered. I explained how every one of us can be like that lantern – a shining light for the Lord Jesus, as we invite the Light of the World to come into our lives, our bodies, and to shine through us. Then we compared the two lanterns. Given the choice, which one would we choose? I suggested that we needed to light them both, turn off all the lights in the hall, and see which one gave us the best light to read by. Under cover of the darkness as the lights were turned off, I removed the shiny clean glass from the good lantern and replaced it with the blackened glass. Then I lit both lanterns, and those children who were able to point, all pointed to the old and battered lantern as the one giving the best light. When the lights were put back on, they all saw that it was the battered old lantern that was the best to read by, not the new and shiny one as they might have expected!

'Children, it doesn't really matter what the outside frame of the lantern looks like, so long as the light is inside, the lantern filled with oil, and the glass polished. If your heart is filled with the love of God, you can shine for Him wherever He puts you, even if people think your body is a bit battered. You can be more use as missionaries where you live than those with perfect bodies whose thoughts and actions make their glasses so dirty that the light cannot shine out!' How good of the Lord! I had to learn to trust Him to give me the inspiration, as well as the physical strength that I needed for each day, for each meeting.

I left for Canada and the USA, for ten weeks of intensive travelling, with a rather different emphasis from the previous tour. This one was not so much one-off meetings and moving on, but rather several meetings in one place to the same group of people over a weekend. To me this appeared to be a more constructive way of building real contacts and conveying several aspects of the missionary needs of the world and the many methods available to meet those needs. It also gave a greater flexibility in accepting strategic opportunities. I visited seven Bible colleges and university campuses across Canada, and then eight across the USA, with four or five meetings at each. In between these there were ten or more women's outreach, evangelistic meetings. During this tour, God helped me to develop a message on 5Ws as a way of presenting missionary challenge – the why? where? what? who? and which? of Missions.

The 'Why?' brought before us God's compassion for the world in all its need, and His command to us 'You give them something to eat' rather than send them away hungry (Mark 6:32-37).

The 'Where?' gave an opportunity for a survey of world need, using a large flannelgraph map of the world, and blocking in the huge area of Muslim influence through North Africa, Middle East, Turkey, Iraq, Iran, Afghanistan, Pakistan and down through Malaysia and Indonesia; the Hindu block in the subcontinent of India; the Buddhist and Confucianist block through Thailand, China and the Far East – thus bringing into focus the 'ten-forty window'. This is a rectangle formed by a line drawn 10 degrees north of the equator, through the Pacific Ocean, back along a line 40 degrees north of the equator, and closed through the Atlantic Ocean, a window enclosing two billion of the least reached peoples in the world, those most needing missionary endeavour.

The 'What?' gave occasion for testimony regarding what is involved in 'being a missionary'; knowing the Lord Jesus as our own personal Saviour, laying everything aside for the privilege of serving Him, being willing to do anything He asks of us (from building a hospital or being brutalised as a prisoner of war, to being a behind-the-scenes secretary), and accepting that the cost involved is 'worth it' because the Master we serve is 'worthy'.

The 'Who?' lent itself to a direct challenge to every Christian to become more deeply involved in mission than ever before in the realm of giving, of going, and supremely of praying, that we must all allow God to 'stir us' profoundly if His task of reaching every creature in every ethnic group throughout the whole world, with the gospel of redeeming love, is to be achieved.

And then fifthly, the 'Which?' – by which means will this be achieved (or 'How?'): by a willingness to allow God to strip us of all that hinders, to fire us with His compassion and love, to fill us with His vision. This was, of course, a quick survey of all that was written in *Living Sacrifice*.

During this tour, I began scribbling thoughts down towards *Living Faith*, the next book in the Four Pillars series. My thoughts began to focus in on the 'Who?' It was at a WEC Easter Convention in London that God first began speaking to my heart along this particular line. That year, the Annual Convention Meeting was held in Westminster Chapel, where nearly 2,000 people poured in. The morning was spent fixing banners to all the galleries, bearing such slogans as 'Up! for this is the day!', 'Now then, do it!', 'Go into all the world and preach the Gospel' and CT Studd's motto across the front, 'If Jesus Christ be God and died for me, then no sacrifice is too great for me to make for Him.' It was an exciting day, but for those of us asked to take part, somewhat intimidating!

I remember that the Chapel had just recently been recarpeted with a lovely deep blue pile carpet. And I was using, as a visual aid, a pot of white gloss paint, a paint brush and a rough piece of wood. Several of my friends prayed earnestly, not just that the message would be acceptable, but possibly more importantly, that I would not drop the paint pot! Starting from *Stir up the gift of God* (2 Tim. 1:6 KJV) and ending with *'And they came, every one whose heart stirred him up, and every one whom his spirit made willing, and they brought the Lord's offering ...'* (Ex.35:21 KJV), and largely based on the old Keswick hymn, 'Stir me, O stir me, Lord .. .Stir me to give, to go, but most to pray ..' (by Mrs A. Head). There were three challenges. The first was to those of us who should be the 'givers' (of cash, yes, but even more importantly, of our talents, our children, our so-called rights), to others of us who could be the 'go-ers' (be it to far away places, cross-culturally, to as yet unreached people groups, or to our near neighbours, often quite as spiritually needy), and thirdly, to all of us, to be the 'pray-ers', to pray without ceasing, to turn every moment and situation of our daily lives into knowledgable prayer, persistent prayer, believing prayer.

I didn't drop the paint pot or splash the precious blue carpet! But I did manage to paint the brown wood white, challenging us all to allow God to stir us up (as old-fashioned paint needed stirring before being used), and to apply us where and how He chose when He knew we were ready. Our task is to be wholly available to Him, and He is responsible for the changes wrought in the hearts of those He is seeking to reach with the gospel.

This message became more and more part of me, and led me to think out the basic message of the next book along those lines – as the application of Faith – faith to give as, what and when God wants, faith to go wherever He directs and, above all, faith to pray, without losing faith if the answer does not come at the moment or in the way that we wish or expect. As I prayed over this, I became more and more convinced that our faith must not depend on the answer to any of those challenges. If we pray earnestly for something specific, and it does not materialise, this must not shake our faith. God may have answered 'No' or 'Wait!' He knows best what we need and when we need it, yet He does desire us to ask Him for it. The struggle to define faith made the writing of the prologue very difficult. What is faith? How is it obtained? How does it work? I kept putting it off, as I developed each of the other chapters.

One Sunday on the tour, I spoke three times in Memphis. At about 11 p.m., I caught a plane to Dallas, where I had to change on to a larger flight to Los Angeles. It was midnight as I walked into the small terminal building for local planes, and everyone else on the plane seemed to know exactly what they were doing and where they were going. I tried to ask one or two people where I should go for my connecting flight, but all were too hurried to help me. Suddenly the lights dimmed as that part of the airport closed down for the night! There was no-one about, just myself, forlornly holding tightly to my briefcase. A cleaner suddenly came up the stairs to collect a cardigan she had left behind. 'Please,' I called out to her, 'Can you help me?' I explained what I wanted. 'Yes,' she answered, 'you need to catch an orange train across to the main airport. Go across there to the elevator. Go down to the first floor then turn right. Go to the bottom of the corridor, turn left and you will reach the platform. Be sure to wait for an *orange* train!' and she was gone.

I made my way across to the elevator. It was pitch dark inside. I found the buttons, and pressed the bottom one for ground floor. Arriving there, I pushed one button higher than the bottom one I could feel, to go back to 'first floor' (having completely forgotten that Americans call ground floor first floor!). I then turned right. But at the bottom of the corridor there was no left turn! I stumbled back to the elevator, and went back to ground floor, realising my mistake. Precious time was going. My flight to Los Angeles was almost due for take-off. I eventually found my way to the platform but between me and the platform there was a grill, and the only way through it was a turnstile that needed a 'quarter' to release it and give me entrance. I did not have a quarter (American equivalence to a 20p piece).

How was I to get through? I hurriedly unpacked my briefcase, pushed all the bits and pieces, including my Bible and file of notes for up-coming talks, under the grill, flattened the briefcase and squeezed it under. Then I climbed the grill, squeezed through between the top and the ceiling, dropped down the other side, refilled my briefcase, and just then a train came in carrying an orange light! I was glad no-one caught me in the act and I trust the USA will not feel I cheated them of a quarter. Clambering on to the train, I hoped it would go fast! It was empty except for me. Arriving at the end of its journey into a fully lighted area, with crowds of hurrying people, I suddenly heard my name called over the loud speaker.

'How do I get to where I need to be?' I gasped, somewhat incoherently, to the first official-looking person I could find. Then, following the directions, I ran ... and made it. The doors of the waiting plane shut behind me as I entered it!

We reached Los Angeles, where I was met by a missionary couple on home assignment from Indonesia, in the early hours of the morning. Together we searched for my luggage, but it had *not* made the flight and was doubtless still sitting in Dallas Airport. They drove me out to Biola University (where I was to be ministering there all week, in the student missionary convention) where they left me with the porter who said he would take me to my room. We walked across the compound, he let me in to one of the girls' dormitory blocks and told me I was in Room H. Making my way down the dark corridor I found the room, went in and switched on the light, only to find an empty room. There was a bedstead but no mattress, let alone blankets or bed linen! I nearly burst into tears. I was tired, hungry, lonely, minus my luggage, and uncertain of what the week had in store for me. I probably dozed off, but wakened at the first sound of people in the corridor outside. Slipping out, I asked, rather sheepishly, 'Can anyone help me, please?'

This was met by an almost stony stare, which seemed to say, 'Whoever are you? and why do you need help?'

'I arrived during the night,' I tried to explain. 'I am your missionary speaker for this week, and my luggage has not come. Could anyone possibly lend me a toothbrush and a comb?'

It must have sounded very stupid and lame. The girls certainly didn't leap to attention to do anything for me, though one did produce the requested articles. When they went for breakfast I followed them. In the dining hall I paused at the registration desk to explain who I was and immediately things began to happen. I explained to the lady who came to help me, and to give me an instruction sheet for the week, that I had arrived during the night, but that my suitcase had failed to come with me. And I mentioned that there was nothing in Room H. She was horrified and said this would be put right at once.

After breakfast, I managed to get to the first meeting where I was to speak to the 1,000 girls gathered in the big hall, on 'Why Missions?' The day wore on till bedtime when I found my bed made up, and a towel and some soap laid out for me. Exhausted, I fell into a deep sleep. Next morning, on the way to breakfast, I met some of the same girls I had spoken to the previous morning.

'Has your suitcase arrived yet?' they asked.

'No!' I laughed. 'While I am still wearing these clothes, you'll know it hasn't come!' And suddenly, their attitude changed.

'Come back with us after breakfast,' they said. We went back

to the dormitory together, and they showered me with gifts:
night attire, a clean blouse, a nice skirt, and one girl brought me
a teddy-bear for my bed!

Then they confided in me. 'We just didn't want another
missionary to come and talk at us! We had all determined not to
listen to you, and not to help you. But yesterday's talk got under
our skin. And you were so uncomplaining, even when we had
meanly emptied your room of all basic necessities. When you
asked us to lend you a toothbrush … that was the end!' We all
roared with laughter together. Suddenly, I found I was accepted,
one of them, and it all happened because I had lost my luggage!

Was God trying to teach me not just to *say* that I believed in
Romans 8:28 '*We know that in all things God works for the good of
those who love him, who have been called according to his purpose*'
but actually *to believe* it. Even lost luggage can be part of God's
overall purpose … if I am willing to see it that way.

The luggage eventually turned up, just in time for me to
leave with it the following Monday morning for Columbia Bible
College. Over the years, I have been to CBC many times, and
I love every visit. They packed my three days with eight or more
opportunities to speak, including talking to the girls in their
sitting-rooms. As usual, their questions included 'How did you
cope with being single?' And they were a bit nonplussed when
I said that singleness is a privileged gift from God, and one that
was to be accepted with both hands. Then, surprisingly, the men
asked me if I would share with them. 'Why should you talk to
the girls and not us?' they wanted to know.

'What do you want me to talk about?' I asked.

'The same as you talked about to the girls!' they replied.

Well, we did discuss some fairly deep questions, particularly
relating to the sufferings that our group of missionaries underwent
during the Congo Rebellion of the 1960s. I shared some of the
horrific stories of what others suffered, especially of one married
man, tied to a tree, who was made to watch those wicked men
rape his wife. 'How does one *then* obey the commandment:

"Love your enemies"? What does that command mean in that sort of context?' I asked. I pray that none of those men will ever have to face such a situation, but should it ever occur, maybe they are a little better prepared to deal with it.

Throughout the ten weeks, there were ten women's outreach meetings. I always shrank from these, saying that I was not naturally an evangelist. That may sound strange coming from a missionary. But all my ministry in Africa had been with Christians, teaching them, building them up in their most holy faith, training them to be evangelists. We always said that all our college graduates were 'medical evangelists', but I myself had very little direct contact with unsaved people. Of course, most of the patients in our hospital were not Christians, but the problem there for me was one of language. We could have 12 or more languages spoken in the wards at any one time, and most of my medical work had to be done through interpreters. I could certainly take ward prayers through an interpreter. Our hospital chaplain, Agoya, was an excellent interpreter. But he was also an excellent evangelist, so it always seemed better that he preached in the wards, while I taught the students.

Now I was faced with the challenge of presenting the gospel, not now to simple nationals in a primitive part of Congo, but to sophisticated, well-educated people in the western world, most of whom had heard the gospel before, and either rejected it or neglected to make a response. This was a different ball-game.

Slowly, over the first three years of deputation ministry, a particular presentation took shape for reaching out to women in these evangelistic efforts, remembering there would be non-Christians there, as well as young believers and probably also mature servants of the Lord. As so often in other situations, I used a flannelgraph to hold their attention – a bicycle wheel, with all its spokes and the hub and the outside rim. The *hub* represented Christ, utterly essential as the pivot around which all else moved. The *spokes* were ourselves, each in our own individual place, rightly related to the hub, and 'well-oiled' to assure smooth running. The *rim* represented each one's little bit of world. The spoke was needed to put the Hub in touch with its bit of world, transferring the strength and power from the Hub to the rim. When the wheel was moving fast, the Hub and the rim could be seen, but the spokes became a blur. Were we willing not to be noticed or thanked, so long as the Hub remained related to the rim?

The whole talk was based on Paul's words to the Christians at Colosse: '*Complete in Him.*' Are we complete *in* Jesus, or incomplete because we have never accepted Him and the wonderful salvation He offers us? Do we run like an un-oiled bicycle, all creaking and rusty, what I called a cr-cr-Christian, always grumbling and complaining! Or are we like a well-oiled bicycle, running smoothly, uncomplaining, even in the face of difficulties? It has been amazing how graciously God has blessed that message in so many different places. I never cease to wonder at God's power to inspire in us new ways of presenting the precious, age-old gospel, to meet the needs of all people everywhere.

Chapter Four

Digging Ditches in Australasia and in Dealing with Hurts

At the close of 1979, *Living Sacrifice*, the first of the series of four books that I was attempting to write for WEC on the Mission's Four Pillars, was actually published, and it was an exciting day for me. I sensed that God was telling me to keep on with the writing ministry, even in the midst of all the speaking engagements. I confess I had no training whatsoever in the techniques of writing, but many friends helped in getting the manuscript ready for publication. The initial scribbling of the proposed contents of each chapter and the overall format was not particularly difficult. But the long process of checking, cutting out, filling in, spelling, construction of sentences and paragraphs ... I found that tedious. Had friends not kept me at it, I would probably never have completed the project. But now it was published and I could turn my mind more fully to *Living Faith*, the next in the series.

I was preparing for a four-month tour of Australasia, from January to April 1980, visiting from Townsville in North Queensland, south to Tasmania, across to New Zealand, westwards to Adelaide and Melbourne, and eventually to Perth. The tour was arranged by three groups planning together: the InterVarsity Students' Christian Unions (UCCF), the Christian Women's Clubs International (CWCI), and my Mission, WEC

International. Then something occurred. With hindsight, it would be easy to say that the devil was not happy, either with the publication of *Living Sacrifice* or with the planned tour of meetings and all the people who would be challenged. It was not so easy to see things like that at the time.

Someone with whom I was staying in the autumn misunderstood my meaning in a certain conversation we had together, and sadly this person was convinced that I had lied. I gave assurance that, not only had I not said what I was believed to have said, but I had not even thought along those lines. I was sad that this friend did not seem to know me well enough to know that I would not lie. And I was hurt by the accusation, possibly more deeply hurt than I realised. I was, of course, afraid that the statement that I had lied would spread rapidly, at least among our mutual friends, and just as the book *Living Sacrifice* was going on sale. I wanted to stop this and to clear my name, to proclaim my innocence of this particular offence.

Then certain events from the past came forcibly back into my mind. During my first year in Congo, I shared the home of my field leader and his wife, Jack and Jessie Scholes. They were like parents to me, helping me to settle in and learn the language and customs of the country. During that year, Jessie became very ill with Black Water Fever and I nursed her for three months. One day, while resting in my room for the midday siesta, a knock at the back door roused me. I slipped my feet into bedroom slippers, and quietly went to open the door, hoping not to waken Jack and Jessie who were also resting. A visiting missionary from another village had come to visit Jack. I gave them both a cup of tea, then left for my afternoon clinic.

During the following week, a letter came from that visitor to Jack. Having read the letter, he sent for me to come to his study, passed it to me and left me to read it. There was a suggestion in the letter that, to a casual observer, my presence *in bedroom slippers* in their home at midday might be misinterpreted as Jack was also resting there. The inference was that there could be a wrong relationship between us. My immediate reaction was one of furious indignation, not that *I* was under suspicion, but that *Jack* was. Jack was the most godly person I have ever met. His life reflected the loveliness of Jesus, and I simply could not bear that anyone could possibly suggest that he might have done or thought anything improper towards me or anyone else. I felt the letter should be destroyed and utterly ignored!

Jack came back into the study, and I burst out, with all the indignation that stirred in my heart. He waited quietly for me to finish my outburst, and then, taking the letter from me, spoke quietly and gently. 'No, Helen,' he said. 'To tear the letter up and ignore the implied criticism is simply one way of declaring "we are innocent", one way of self-vindication.' Hardly listening to his further explanation, I said: 'But we *are* innocent! The inferred criticism is grossly unfair and untrue!' 'I know, I know,' Jack agreed patiently, 'but "Vengeance belongeth to the Lord!" We don't have to vindicate ourselves. Leave the Lord to work that out in His own way and time. Wouldn't it be better if we found you another house to live in, and so silence any such implied criticism, whether true or untrue?'

It was beyond me! I felt such a course of action was tantamount to agreeing that the accuser had a point. But I accepted Jack's suggestion, believing strongly that he always spoke prayerfully and with much deeper wisdom and maturity than I had. I left their lovely home and went to live in a couple of rooms in what was known as the Guest House. I went over and over Jack's reasoning, asking the Lord to help me accept and believe what he had said. I looked up all the Bible references about taking vengeance and about self-vindication.

Starting with 1 Peter 2:21-23: '*To this you were called, because Christ suffered for you, leaving you an example, that you should follow in his steps. "He committed no sin, and no deceit was found in his mouth." When they hurled their insults at him, he did not retaliate; when he suffered, he made no threats. Instead, he entrusted himself to him who judges justly.*' I then turned to

Deuteronomy 32:35, and to where this is quoted in the New Testament in Romans 12:19-21: '*Do not take revenge, my friends, but leave room for God's wrath, for it is written: "It is mine to avenge; I will repay," says the Lord. On the contrary: "If your enemy is hungry, feed him; if he is thirsty, give him something to drink. In doing this you will heap burning coals on his head." Do not be overcome by evil, but overcome evil with good.*'

The more I read and prayed over these words, the more I saw that Jack lived them. But I found it unbelievably hard to want to give myself wholly to implementing them. Certainly from that time on, it was implanted deeply in my heart and mind that 'Vengeance belongs to the Lord'. That must mean that we are not to indulge in self-justification.

Shortly after that episode, there was another occurrence that underlined the principle involved. Ninety miles south of Nebobongo, on the other side of the gold-mine mountain range, there was a small forest village where WEC missionaries had laboured for many years to establish a church among the WaBari people. A couple there were expecting their first child. It had been arranged that I would go to stay with them and see the young wife safely through the birth. However, I then had a sharp attack of malaria, complicated by jaundice. Jack sent a runner to Buambi, to tell the couple the situation and suggest that they make their way north to Nebobongo, where the mother could be given all the care she needed. A somewhat abrupt reply came back, stating that they had no available means of transport, and reminding me of my promise to be available to them. Jack discussed this with me and I agreed to go. But I was angry as I considered their response was selfish, as they seemed to have given no thought to what that journey would mean to me, still weak from three weeks of sickness.

Jack knew exactly what was going on in my heart, and he remonstrated with me. 'I want to ask you to do something – not for me, not even entirely for yourself, but chiefly for Christ's sake. Go to them. Do all you can for them AND do not make too much of your illness. Just die to yourself, Helen, and the Lord will bless you. If you can accept that to this young couple down there in forest-land, your delay has caused ·distress and anxiety, God will help you go to them in humility and to ask their forgiveness for causing that distress.' Is this what the Bible means by 'going the second mile'? Somewhere, deep down in my heart, a chord had been struck though my rebellious anger sought to stifle it. I suppose I knew Jack was right, but I did not want to acknowledge it. I wanted the right to be angry and to proclaim my innocence of any implied accusation of negligence of duty.

God won that round. He taught me, and I learned slowly. That God did not always allow us to defend ourselves (or even each other) in certain circumstances, seemed hard to me, particularly if someone had clearly been wrongly accused or misjudged. Christ, for my sake, was misunderstood by His closest friends, and falsely accused by His enemies, yet He made no effort no defend Himself. '*As a sheep before her shearers is silent, so he did not open his mouth*' (Is. 53:7). Was I willing to so love God, with all my heart, that I would give up loving myself, and my reputation, and the importance of what others thought of me?

Sadly, I was slow to learn, and God in His patient mercy was willing to teach me the same lesson over and over again. Many years after this episode, when I was working far away from our Mission area, at Nyankunde, an inter-mission medical centre, one of our WEC missionaries from Nebobongo visited me, partly for her own need of medical care, partly for a break from her heavy work-schedule. On her return to our WEC area of service, she reported to Jack 'certain goings on' at Nyankunde, that she had heard of, in which she understood that I was involved, and which seemed to her definitely contrary to our WEC principles. Jack wrote to me for clarification, and I was hurt. Should he not have trusted me, and known that I would not contravene a basic biblical principle in my service to the Congolese, even if others around me felt that it was in order for them to take the line of action that was being criticised? And anyway, why hadn't the missionary spoken to me first, to clarify whether I was involved or not?

My 'hurt' very easily turned to anger. I wrote a sharp letter to defend myself, to criticise the other missionary's action, and to expose Jack's lack of faith in me. Sadly, that was self-justification on a fairly large scale! But wasn't that reasonable action to take? However, I did not have peace in my heart, and I struggled for several days over the issue. At last, I wrote another letter of apology to Jack for the anger in my heart that prompted the first one, but I hadn't dealt with the anger in my heart towards the other missionary.

Not long after this, Jessie had to bring her husband Jack to Nyankunde for major surgery and they stayed in my home. I had the opportunity to love them and serve them, as they had done for me 20 years earlier when I first arrived in Congo. It was a privilege. They were just so loving and uncomplaining. Jack was found to have cancer of the head of the pancreas, and there was little the surgeons could do for him except relieve the immediate cause of pain. I nursed him for a month, until he was able to return to Ibambi for his last few weeks before he died. During their stay with me, we talked through all my reactions to the accusation levelled against me. Jack gently assured me that he had never doubted my integrity, but had merely sought to give me the opportunity of an honest and simple explanation of the misunderstanding that had arisen, an explanation that he could then have shown to the other person. Why could I not learn? '"It is mine to avenge: I will repay," says the Lord.'

Yet again, years later, as I mentioned in the prologue, when I wrote to the Congo Leadership, offering to return for three years to teach in the Pastors' School, and I received no reply, I was hurt. Throughout the years the Lord had sought to teach me that, when I am 'hurt', I can be fairly sure that 'I' have got in the way of God's dealings, either with me or through me to others. If my 'I' was truly crucified with Christ, and I was truly indwelt by Jesus, He may indeed be *grieved* by wrongdoing, or false accusations, or misunderstandings by others who should have known better, but He will not be 'hurt'.

In 1979, when I was accused of lying by someone who should have known better (as I thought), just as I was preparing to leave for a long tour of meetings on the other side of the world, I was hurt once again. As I sought to commit the matter to the Lord, all these past occasions welled up in my mind. I knew God was saying to me, yet again, in His infinite patience, 'Trust Me. Leave the whole affair with Me.'

As we approached Christmas, this person rang my friend Pat at home, and asked her how she could continue to be my friend, knowing I had lied. Pat was ready to jump to my defence. When Pat and I had discussed the whole situation previously, I explained as nearly as I could what had actually occurred, and the conversation we had had. Really it was not hard to see how a misunderstanding could have happened, but the person was unwilling to concede there was any possibility of a misunderstanding, remaining adamant that the conversation was remembered verbatim. There was, therefore, no room for any explanation. The letter I sent asking for forgiveness if I had given any cause for misunderstanding was rejected. It was not accepted as a valid apology because it contained no acceptance of the fact that I had lied.

Pat accepted unquestioningly my explanation, and was assured that I had not, either intentionally or unintentionally, lied, but simply that something somewhere had been misinterpreted and misunderstood. So, when the phone call came complaining about my attitude, and my unwillingness to apologise, Pat was ready to leap to my defence. 'No, Pat, please don't!' I remonstrated. 'We must leave it to the Lord. We must not justify ourselves, nor can we justify one another. Vengeance belongs to the Lord.' Somehow, it is easier to accept that for oneself, but much harder to accept it for a loved one. It hurts so much more when someone you love is falsely accused. That is what Jack Scholes tried to teach me all those years ago. I could not defend him, any more than I could defend myself.

I packed and left for Australia with this unresolved burden in my heart. When I arrived at our WEC Headquarters in Sydney, I was told there were a few more meetings booked than had been on the list they had sent me. Of immediate importance was a series of meetings at Canberra University, for the Executive Members of all the University Christian Unions across the length and breadth of the country. They always met together in early January for teaching and fellowship to prepare them for the ministry of the new year. Michael Baughen was to give a series of five or six Bible studies on prayer, and I was asked to give three addresses of missionary challenge. I spent the weekend trying to sort out my material and prepare for those very strategic meetings with some 200 students.

Arriving at the Canberra University Campus, I found I was sharing a very nice duplex with Michael and his wife in the other half. At the fourth of his Bible studies, when he was speaking about praying for those who hurt us, persecute us, or hate us, I sat at the back of the auditorium thinking, 'Well, I don't have anyone like that. I don't hate anyone,' when suddenly the whole recent 'saga' leapt into my mind.

'Lord, this person may have accused me falsely, but I don't hate!' I tried to say. 'Do you pray for this person?' the Lord nudged me. 'Well, no, I don't.' Could I? I didn't want to think about it, but I couldn't get the thought out of my mind. No, I did not pray for this person, and because of what had occurred, I did not really want to. I slipped out of the meeting during the singing of the last hymn and went back to our apartment to wait for Michael. I needed his help to deal with the self-righteous attitude in my heart. I boiled a kettle, got a tea tray ready for the three of us, and waited. Eventually there was a knock at the door, and a second-year engineering student was there. I brought her in, gave us both tea, presuming she also wanted to talk to Michael.

'Sorry Michael is so long in coming,' I said to her. 'Is there anything I can do for you?' 'Oh,' she said, 'I haven't come to see Michael, but you.' I was embarrassed at having kept her sitting there waiting. 'Sorry,' I said, 'what can I do to help you?' 'No,' she replied, '*I* don't need anything, but I felt the Lord wanted me to come to ask you if I could do anything to help *you*. All this week you have looked so unhappy!' Amazed and humbled, I began to share a little bit of what was causing me such unease, and about which I was indeed unhappy.

And as I talked to her, suddenly I realised what God was trying to say to me. I almost laughed! 'Thank you, dear' I blurted out. 'I think I understand what the Lord is trying to say to me!' She obviously didn't, and I attempted to explain. When we were captured by guerrilla soldiers in the civil war in the 1960s, we never really felt hatred towards them. Even when folk asked us how could we forgive them for what they did to us, we were honestly puzzled by the question, as we had not thought in terms of needing to forgive them. We had known they were not Christians, that they urgently needed to be saved and to be forgiven by God (not us). In a way, that had been an easy lesson to learn and had left no particular scars.

But now, I believed the Lord was inviting me, in some very small measure, to understand a little more fully what the fellowship of sharing in His suffering might mean. Had He, our Lord and Saviour Jesus Christ, not been betrayed by one of His closest friends, one of His inner circle, when Judas kissed Him in the Garden of Gethsemane? And one outstanding factor in the trial scene leading up to Christ's crucifixion was that He, the Son of God, made no effort to resist or to justify Himself. Rather, we see the perfect fulfilment of what Peter says of Him: '*To this you were called, because Christ suffered for you, leaving you an example, that you should follow in his steps. "He committed no sin, and no deceit was found in his mouth." When they hurled their insults at him, he did not retaliate; when he suffered he made no threats. Instead, he entrusted himself to him who judges justly*' (1 Pet. 2:21-23).

I don't think that lovely young student really followed all that I was trying to say, but I thanked her earnestly for coming to see me and for obeying the Lord's prompting. After she left, I went to my room and wrote a letter to the person concerned, asking forgiveness for having harboured hard feelings, and also for anything in our conversation that fateful evening that could have made possible the misunderstanding of what I was actually trying to say. I was about to stick the aerogramme up and address it, when I was assailed by an urgent sense that something wasn't right. In fact, I was convinced that I was not to send the letter. Why ever not? I was so sure that I would have peace of heart once the letter was written. I felt I could almost be joyous at last for the first time for three months! Now what was wrong?

I sat and prayerfully re-read what I had written, and the Lord enabled me to realise that this very letter was a subtle way of surreptitiously vindicating myself. The person concerned had no idea that I had hard thoughts, or that I felt that they were in the wrong about what had occurred. I was feeding such thoughts in my letter in order to vindicate myself. In other words, I was practically saying, in a veiled way, that I had no reason to ask for forgiveness as I considered myself free of fault, that no-one had any real justification in demanding me to seek forgiveness from them. That may sound extraordinarily convoluted reasoning (and grammar, but that is to preserve the anonymity of the person concerned), and I certainly hadn't thought it all out like that. But I came to see that was the implication of what I had written, and I knew God was asking me to tear up the letter, and not to send it. I tore it up, and then I had an intense consciousness of peace.

That was the beginning of a long and fairly exhausting but very exciting tour of meetings. From the beautiful capital city of Australia up to the heights of the Blue Mountains to the Keswick Conference Centre for a Youth Convention, with four meetings of 800 young people. It rained almost all weekend, and the convenors were thrilled. Because of the heavy rain the young folk came to all the meetings (it was dry in the hall!) instead of going off walking or playing ball games in the grounds. I can still remember how delighted I was when a crowd of them responded to the challenge to be willing to go wherever the Lord might call them.

From there I travelled north to Townsville in Queensland, and was it hot! The dry heat, touching on 40 degrees centigrade, was something I had never experienced before. At the morning meeting in the Salvation Army Hall all the fans were going in an attempt to make it bearable. Folk started coming in, some having travelled huge distances to get there. I was trying to find a way to fix my flannelgraph visual aid so that it would not be blown off the board by the air currents from the fans when, suddenly, there was a power cut! Certainly the flannelgraph was happy, but the heat in the hall was almost unbearable, especially as we slowly packed in nearly 300 people. Bless them, they endeavoured both to sing and to listen. Then, as suddenly as it had gone off, the power came on again.

Through Rockhampton, I travelled to Brisbane then south to Tasmania, and seven meetings with the students at our WEC Missionary Training College. One afternoon, as I was driven by a friend on the College staff to see the locality, we passed through places with wonderful Cornish names. My friend didn't know that I was of Cornish origin, and I could hardly believe I wasn't home again! Then we came to a village, in the centre of which there was an old wooden building with its name proudly carved in a wooden beam, 'Roseveare's Inn'. I was told that one of my ancestors had come across with the first convict ship to Hobart in the south of the island to open an inn to serve the prison warders on their days off!

Following a women's meeting one morning in Ulverston, a lady asked me over the luncheon, 'Did you notice the mirror in …'s room?' and she named the child in whose bedroom I had slept that night. Strange question. I thought a moment, and replied, 'Quite honestly, no.' I had noticed all the toys, dolls, teddy-bears, and numerous creatures with wobbly eyes, but I could not recall the mirror. What was special about it, I wondered? I went back to the same home the next evening, and I looked carefully, but really there was nothing special to note. Puzzled, I pondered why the questioner had asked me about it. Then a line of thought came to me, and I believe the Lord was opening my eyes to a new perspective.

When we look in a mirror, we don't really want to see the mirror at all, but our image in the mirror. In fact, we probably only notice the mirror itself if it is dirty – splashed with toothpaste or misted up – so that we cannot see our face clearly. God wants our lives to mirror the loveliness of the life of Christ. We, as Christians, want others to see Jesus in us rather than looking at ourselves. In fact, if people notice us, and remember us in any detail, it almost certainly means that we have been in the way of their seeing Jesus. Any sin, any 'dirt' in my life, will hinder others seeing a clear reflection of Jesus.

As I thought this through, I was reminded of a lovely illustration of this same truth, from my early days in Congo. I had been invited by one of the church catechists to cycle with him to visit a native gold-mine in the southern mountains. Doubtless that was illegal, in those colonial days, and so well-hidden from public view. Arriving in the crater area, where all the palm trees had been cleared away, we saw this lake of boiling gold. Men, stripped to the waist, pouring with sweat, stoked the firing holes of an underground kiln. The worst impurities had already been drained away and this was the final purification method, the 'blowing off' of any residual impurity as exploding gas. To one side, there remained one solitary palm tree.

'Why the one tree?' I asked. 'I'll show you!' and the guide crossed over to the solitary palm, shinned up to the top fronds, and called out to a colleague, 'Haul!' I then noticed a liana-rope stretching from the top of the palm tree to a tree stump on the opposite side of the lake of molten gold. As an African hauled on the rope, the palm tree, with our guide precariously hanging on, bent down over the surface of the lake. 'OK!' and the helper slowly released the rope: the palm stood up erect, and our guide came down and crossed to us. 'What on earth were you doing?' I gasped. 'I am the watchman,' he explained. 'So what?' I demanded. And then came his explanation – so simple, so amazing – though I have never checked its scientific veracity.

'When I look down from above, while there are any impurities left in the gold the boiling surface is continually erupting in vast exploding bubbles, and I can see nothing clearly. But when the gold is absolutely pure, when I look down from above I can see the unruffled reflection of my face because the surface is completely still!'

As we cycled back home, I thought through that picture and realised that God is purifying our lives by continually stoking His kiln, to keep our inner selves, as it were, boiling. When the process is complete He will be able to see the unruffled reflection of His face in us. Isn't that the same as saying that the surface of my mirror must be absolutely clean so that others see Jesus, rather than me, when they look at me?

Chapter Five

Digging More Ditches in Australasia and Dealing with Suffering

From Tasmania, I returned to Sydney for one night in the airport hotel, before flying over to New Zealand. But by the time I disembarked in Auckland, I knew I was sick. I really felt wretched. Actually, I often became airsick on flights, but this seemed worse than usual. It turned out to be the beginning of ten miserable days, possibly as a result of a mild form of food poisoning. The lady who met me and took me to her home to have tea before our first meeting was immensely patient with me. She had prepared a wonderful feast for my arrival but I was completely unable to touch it. Somehow we struggled through the five booked meetings with over 400 women at the CWCI Auckland Convention. I guess Mrs Betty must have been glad when WEC collected me! The whole of the next ten days became a blur; I just managed to stay upright for the duration of each meeting before having to lie down until the next one. I travelled south through North Island, across to South Island, and as far as Dunedin then back again to UCCF meetings in the University of Auckland and missed all the beauty of that wonderful land, but just managed not to have to cancel any booked meetings.

When I eventually reached the Stanwell Tops Convention Centre in New South Wales, I felt well again and able to cope with the programme. It was following a women's convention in

Belgrave Heights, near Melbourne, that the next 'ditch' had to be dug. Some 2,000 women gathered in the large canvas hall for their annual gathering, prepared to hear God's Word and to be encouraged for the next year of service for the Master.

At the end of the Saturday morning session, as I was leaving the tent to make my way across to the dining hall, a little lady sitting in one of the pews, lightly touched me on the arm. 'Would you have time to help me?' she whispered. I felt guilty at having been in such a hurry that I had not really noticed her. Sitting down, I smiled encouragingly at her. 'Five months ago,' she started, 'my two-and-a-half year old son was drowned in our family swimming pool.' I immediately felt choked up; I could just feel her pain. I put an arm round her and waited for her to continue. 'My 'Christian' friends told me to praise the Lord,' she said. And as she spoke, I felt a rising anger in my heart. How could anyone speak like that to a young mother in the midst of her grief, possibly with guilt feelings too? Maybe they had left the gate open or some other such thing? I just knew that my loving heavenly Father would never have demanded praise from her in those circumstances.

'And when I could not praise God,' she continued, 'they told me I must have sin in my heart.' I cried out to God, asking Him to tell me what to say to this little mother. 'Not in the future, Lord, I need Your help right now!' But all that came into my mind was a sudden clear picture of the night I was taken captive by the guerrillas in Congo, nearly twenty years before. What was the connection? Why did the Lord remind me of that night in these circumstances? I knew that God had spoken to me that night in several different ways, but what exactly had He said? 'Please, God,' I prayed, 'tell me clearly now. What do You want me to share with Marge?'

As I was forced at gun point along the corridor of my home, there at Nebobongo, in 1964, the Lord told me that those evil men were not beating me, but seeking to beat Him in me. All He was asking of me was the loan of my body. Then He had seemed to add, 'Can you thank Me?' God was not asking me to thank Him for the evil; we never thank God for evil. We only thank Him for what He gives us, and He never gives us evil, even though He may permit us to go through evil. 'Can you thank Me for trusting you?' He seemed to ask. What an amazing thought! I can understand *me* trusting *Him*, but I had never thought of Him trusting me. So 'Can you thank Me for trusting you with this experience, even if I never tell you why?' was what the Lord had put in my heart and mind to share with those students at Twin City Bible Church in Urbana, just two years before!

I thought back quickly to that experience. Not only had it been terrifying and horrific, but also amazing and humbling, in the middle of that long-ago night, as I came to realise that God, who could have stopped the situation developing, who could have taken me out of it all, who could have prevented it going on, actually chose to trust me to go through it with Him as some part of His greater plan. It had seemed as though He was trying to reassure me that someone would be blessed, somehow, somewhere, at some future date. I had managed to stumble out, 'OK, God, though I don't understand how anyone can be blessed by this nightmare.' I was so sure that we were all going to be killed, and that no-one would ever know what we had suffered first. 'But if this is part of Your wonderful overall plan, Lord,' I prayed, 'yes, I thank You for trusting me to go through it.' Immediately, despite the pain and horror, there was an immense peace, right in the midst of the terror and pain.

I shared a little of all this with Marge, and asked her if she could thank God for trusting her with this tragic event, even if He never told her why. At first, she seemed to shut off from me; it seemed such a preposterous suggestion. It was almost as awful as those who just said, 'Praise the Lord!' But it wasn't. It was subtly different. Rather than being a blind, almost meaningless, use of words, it was actually a thought-out statement of faith, that God cannot deliberately inflict evil on us. He has promised to give us all good and needful things out of His glorious riches in Christ Jesus. But if He, Almighty God, believes we are ready to be entrusted with a deeper level of sharing in the fellowship of His sufferings, that we are ready to trust Him utterly when everything seems to cry out against such a trust, then yes, we can thank Him for trusting us in such a manner, and so allow Him to guide us through the pain.

Eventually Marge reached through the darkness of her grief, and she prayed through her streaming tears, 'OK, God, I don't understand You. I don't see where there can be blessing in this. But I want to thank You for trusting me with this tragedy.' We hugged each other and we wept together for a short time, then together we thanked God for the restored peace in our hearts. Three years later, when I was back in that part of Australia for more meetings, I stood in the doorway of a Baptist church shaking hands with people as they left. A lovely, bright-faced lady came towards me, her hand outstretched. 'You don't remember me, do you?' I certainly did; it was Marge! 'I've prayed for you every day for the past three years,' I assured her.

Then she told me the sequel to that story. Marge returned home from the Convention in March 1980, to share my words to her with her husband. At first he did not want to hear. But eventually the day came, when, together, the two of them knelt together and said, 'Thank You, Lord, for trusting us with this tragedy. Please work out Your perfect will through it.' They then knew a wonderful inner peace. Later that very week, Marge told me, 'a child ran out of a garden lower down our road, and was killed by a passing car. The parents were not Christians. In fact, they were of another faith. But because they saw how we had been helped to come to terms with the death of our son, they let us comfort them. During these past three years, first the mother, and now also the father, have come to faith in Jesus!' I praised the Lord with her. How gracious of Him, that He should let us see and understand at least something of the 'Why?' So many, many times in the succeeding years the Lord has given me opportunities to share that word from Himself with others. 'Can you thank Me for trusting you with this experience, even if I never tell you why?'

It was also during that first tour of meetings in Australia that I was asked repeatedly by women, 'Why does a God of love allow such suffering?' I took it that they meant 'Why did God allow you missionary women to suffer the appalling brutalities and savagery that you went through in the civil war in Congo?' Hadn't we given our all to serve Him? 'Why didn't He protect you?' they asked. I felt there was almost an implied criticism of God, as though He had treated us badly in allowing us to go through a certain amount of suffering. I began to put my thoughts on paper in order to seek to answer this searching question. This exercise proved to be a tremendous blessing to me. As I have shared these thoughts with many other groups in the past twenty years, I have seen God bless so many so richly, often liberating them from feelings of bitterness or hardness of heart towards God, and also from the syndrome of 'pity me' which can so easily blight our spiritual lives when we let it take over.

It seems to me that the question, 'Why does a God of love allow suffering?' is a contradiction in itself. It is *because* God is a God of love that He allows suffering. When we think back to the beginning of all things, we know 'God is.' That ever-present-tense God created humans to be His friends, who would love, worship and serve Him. If we are to love Him, we have to be free to choose to do so. Love by compulsion is not true love. The very fact that He created us with the freedom to choose to love Him means that we had to be free to choose *not* to love Him. God knew that some would do just that. So He was faced with the awful dilemma of how to bring someone back into relationship with Himself, someone who had freely chosen to break that relationship. So (as I understand the Scriptures) before God ever created us, He planned our redemption. He knew from the start of time there would be the necessity for His beloved Son to die in our place.

From earliest time, in the Garden of Eden, man was given a simple command to obey, in order to show that he chose to love God. At the same time, he was told the consequence of disobedience, disobedience that would show that he loved himself more than God. *The Lord God commanded the man, "You are free to eat from any tree in the garden; but you must not eat from the tree of the knowledge of good and evil, for when you eat of it, you will surely die"* (Gen. 2:16,17).

So God ordained from the start of life that: '*The wages of sin is death*' (Rom.6:23). Man chose to disobey that first simple command, and so deserved to die physically and to die spiritually, to be separated from God eternally. God knew that the only way of redeeming man was for someone to accept man's deserved wages in his place, that is, for a substitute to be found to die instead of man. But that substitute would have to be without sin, otherwise he would have to die for his own sin and would be unable to die for the sin of others. But who was there without sin? '*For all have sinned and fall short of the glory of God*' (Rom. 3:23). In fact, earlier in the same chapter, we read, '*There is no-one righteous, not even one*' (Rom. 3:10).

The only One without sin is God Himself. So God planned for His own beloved Son to become flesh and to dwell among us men, in order to die in our place, as our perfect substitute. God *planned* the death of His Son '*before the creation of the world*' (Eph.1:4). Why? He did it because He loved us! It was because of His love that God Himself suffered for us. God actually planned His own suffering because of His deep love for us. True love always leads to heart suffering. '*For God so loved the world that He gave His one and only Son, that whoever believes in Him shall not perish but have eternal life*' (John 3:16).

I can think of so many examples of this. True, they are only pale reflections of God's great love and intense suffering as His only Son became sin for us, '*so that in Him we might become the righteousness of God*' (2 Cor. 5:21). Hugh, a 17-year-old student nurse, recently saved, who was willing to give his life to protect me from death at the hands of rebel soldiers, because he loved me. Then there was Pastor Agoya, who was brutally beaten up, when blows were aimed at me, during those same days. And there was a missionary's teenage son, who saw his father savagely murdered by gunmen, who prayed that evening, 'Father, forgive the soldiers who shot my daddy. They did not know what they were doing!'

In each example, it is because of love that the victim is willing to suffer. A mother yearning over a teenager hooked on drugs, or a wife knowing that her husband has failed to gain merited promotion because of his Christian testimony, would not suffer if they did not love. So when I faced the horror of the shame and the cruelty of the guerrilla soldiers, and God whispered to me, 'Can you thank Me for trusting you with this experience, even if I never tell you why?' He made it possible for me, by His overwhelming love, to accept the suffering. The amazing thought that He was offering me the privilege of sharing in some tiny way in the fellowship of His suffering was tremendous. Even at the time, even in the midst of the pain, God actually gave me His peace. And He took away from me, straight away, any desire to question Him or to ask, 'God, why?' I don't honestly think we can answer the question, '*Why* does a God of love allow suffering?' But we can accept from Him the enabling not to ask the question!

There have been opportunities to share these thoughts many times in subsequent years, and not just using the phrase, 'Can you thank Me for trusting you with this experience?' as though it were a charm or mantra, but sincerely moving through to that level of trust in our heavenly Father that can bring complete deliverance and peace. I remember one night at a Bible college in Central Canada, I was on an extensive tour of meetings right across Canada, from Vancouver in the west to St John's, New Brunswick in the east, arranged jointly by Nell Maxwell of 'Women Alive' and my Mission through our Headquarters in Toronto. A very distressed young lady came to my room one night about 11 p.m. after a public meeting in a Bible school in Saskatchewan, asking if I could help her. She told me that, as a young teenager, she had been raped, and that she had been helped by her family and their doctor to 'accept' the trauma.

She had done so, to the best of her ability, and sought to put the matter behind her. Quite recently, she had married a good man. 'But I cannot bear for him to approach me! I freeze. The whole past rises up and frightens me! Can you help me, please?' she sobbed. 'I accepted the past, but I can't get rid of it!'

In those sort of moments, I feel like Joseph before Pharaoh, or Daniel before Nebuchadnezzar. 'No, I'm not sure that I can help you,' I said, 'but I know One who certainly can!' It was in this lady's repeated use of the verb 'accepted', that I sensed the problem lay. When we 'accept' bitterness or hurt or any other wrong inflicted on us by another person, we may lock the skeleton of the incident into a cupboard, and try to lose the key. But in the cupboard, with the skeleton, there is also a small grain of blaming God. When we unlock the cupboard, take out the skeleton, and looking straight into the eyes of our loving heavenly Father, thank Him for trusting us with the experience, even if He never tells us why, then He can free us completely from the pain, and remove from our heart even the tiniest grain of 'blaming Him' for having allowed the experience to occur. It is impossible to blame God at the same time as thanking Him!

As we moved through the planned tour of meetings in Australia in 1980, there were one or two lovely experiences that God allowed to encourage me to know that *He* was in charge, and that I could trust Him each step of the way. I think it was in Port Lincoln we had the first of the day's meetings at a women's rally, with the CWCI. I shared with the ladies, using the flannelgraph of the bicycle wheel, starting by explaining how I had come to know the Lord as my own personal Saviour through seeing a bicycle wheel padlocked to iron railings outside a church in Cambridge, when the thief had stolen the rest of the bike! Then years later, in the heart of Africa, having stopped for a coffee break on the long 300 mile journey from Kampala (Uganda) to Bunia (Congo), I was accosted by a herdsman, with the request, 'Are you a sent-one to tell me of something called Jesus?' Having shared the Scriptures with this man, with the use of the Wordless

Book, I had the enormous privilege of pointing him to Jesus and explaining to him how he could accept the Lord as his Saviour. We prayed together and his face filled with a new-found joy.

As I went back to my car, an African cyclist passed by on his way to the local market, with a huge head of bananas on the carrier. At that precise moment, the hub of the front wheel of his bicycle gave way, and the man fell off. Man, bicycle and bananas spread across the road. Together we helped him up, repaired his bicycle, restored the bananas to him, and saw him on his way. I then turned to the herdsman, and told him *my* story of the bicycle wheel, padlocked to iron railings, that had been the start of my journey to salvation. The herdsman loved it. Africans are very quick to see and appreciate such picture language. And I drove away on my journey homewards, thanking God for His infinite goodness in making me stop at that particular clump of bushes, to meet with that particular man that particular day.

Having shared this story in the morning meeting at the Port Lincoln Women's Convention, everyone went back to their homes for their midday meal. When they returned to the town hall for the afternoon meeting, one group was brimming over with excitement, longing to share with me – and anyone else who would listen! – an amazing event. As they were walking home that midday, suddenly they had seen, bowling down the high street, unaided and alone, a bicycle wheel! Whether its hub was intact or not, I do not know! They just couldn't believe their eyes. But it really reinforced the story they had heard only that morning, and they said, 'We shall never forget that illustration!'

It was nearly at the end of that four months' tour that I reached Albany, in the southwest of Australia. At the rally there I was presented, not only with a beautiful bunch of flowers, but also with a very special gift that I have treasured ever since. It is a lovely little presentation box containing a silver spoon specially fashioned as a Kangaroo Paw, the emblem of the State. The spoon had been crafted by a master silversmith as a presentation gift for the Queen. But, I was told, they always make two on such occasions in case anything goes wrong with one of them, and I had been chosen as recipient of the second! I felt so enormously honoured that I have never used the spoon. It is still in its lovely presentation case. That was such a lovely climax to my first visit to the other side of the world.

At another meeting during a further visit to Australia three years later, in a large church with many university students in the congregation, I challenged them to ask what was holding them back from accepting the Lord's call to missionary service. At the close of my message, the pastor again challenged them all to ask what was holding them back from responding to the Lord's invitation to commit their lives to full-time service for Him? He made a few suggestions such as, to the girls, 'Are you asking the Lord to let you get married first?' and to the fellows, 'Can I just complete a second degree course first, so as to have added security for my future?' Then he said, 'As we sing our closing hymn, if you are willing to give that 'thing' – whatever it is, that is holding you back from total commitment to God – to Him, then would you just come forward as we sing? Don't tell me what the 'thing' is, but be willing to tell God, and to hand it over to Him without reservation!'

As we sang the last hymn, and a few came forward to the front, I watched three young girls sitting in the front row at my right. They appeared to be about 15, 13 and 11 years old. The middle one looked as though she would have liked to come forward, but did not. As the service closed, I went down to speak to her. But the three saw me coming, and bolted out of a side door! So I sat down where they had been, and turned to speak to the ladies in the row behind. One of them was quietly crying. I spoke to the others first, and then turned to her and asked if I could be of any help.

As she spoke, the lady's voice told me at once that she was an American rather than an Australian. She and her husband had gone to Australia a year before as missionaries to the aboriginal peoples. 'We have two daughters,' she said. 'The 15-year-old has fitted straight into her new school and is enjoying our new life here. But the 13-year-old ...' and her voice trembled. With tears flowing, she continued, 'She has completely changed her character. She is tearing our family apart. Even at school she is causing trouble. We just don't know what to do to help her!' Then she asked me, 'Are we wrong to force our children to follow us, even though we are so sure of our calling to be missionaries here?' Then she added, possibly by way of explanation, 'Back home, we lived on Grandma's farm, and she had a horse.'

I was unsure how to answer the question she had asked, and as I was praying for direction, two of the three girls arrived at the end of the pew. I just guessed that one of them would be the 13- year-old. I greeted them both, 'Good evening!' One said a polite, 'Good evening!' The other said, 'Hi!' The first was obviously a local Australian girl, the second an American. I chatted for a moment with the Australian, and then turned to the American. 'You don't belong here, do you?' 'No!' was the short, sharp answer. She had no intention of being drawn into conversation. I tried again, 'It's not easy living in someone else's country, is it?' Again, an abrupt 'No!'

We carried on a monosyllabic conversation for a short while, and I was beginning to feel frustrated, unable to break through her resistance. Then the pastor sent someone to call me to go to the back of the church to talk to some students. A short time later I returned to the church to collect my Bible, and the 13- year- old met me in the aisle. 'Was I too young to come out tonight?' she asked me bluntly. 'No! Did you want to?' 'Yes!' 'OK,' I said, 'Let's go out together now.' So we went together to the low steps at the front of the church and knelt side by side. 'You just tell the Lord Jesus what it is that you want to give to Him,' I encouraged. There was a silence, and then she began to sob. I repeated my suggestion and waited quietly. Then, with tears running down her face, she burst out, 'My horse!' 'That's lovely, dear,' I said, suppressing any surprise. 'Let's just give the horse to Jesus.' We prayed together, as she gave her beloved horse to the Lord.

With a radiant smile, through her tears, she turned to me and said, 'My mum and dad aren't half going to be pleased. I've made their lives hell!' 'And now are you determined to change that?' I asked. 'Yes! Yes indeed. I just want to make their lives heaven, and to help them to be the missionaries they want to be!' She was just 13, but she had known what she was holding on to that was spoiling her life and making her family so unhappy. I wonder how many of us have hidden 'horses' in our lives that we don't want to give up to the Lord.

Chapter Six

Digging Ditches Amongst UK Schoolgirls

There had to be a tremendous switch in gears before the next year of ministry started. The Girl Crusaders' Union (GCU) approached WEC International, my missionary society, to ask if they would 'lend' me to them for a year to head up what they were calling, a 'Forward Movement'. GCU came into being in 1915 during the First World War, when a group of ladies became burdened for schoolgirls they saw, especially on Sunday afternoons, wandering aimlessly on the streets with no-one apparently caring about them. Encouraged by some Christian men who, a few years earlier, had started Crusaders – Sunday afternoon Bible Classes for schoolboys – they took the plunge and brought into being the GCU. The idea caught on, and in a very short time classes opened all over the south of England, then in the north, across into Ireland, up to Scotland and eventually in Wales. A Council was formed to safeguard the aim of the Union, which was to teach the Bible in such a way that girls came to a knowledge of the Saviour and grew in their faith into mature Christian women. A badge could be earned by attending ten classes, and a Bible was presented to any girl who attended a further 50 classes. A regular magazine was started and Easter and summer camps organised. Inter-class activities and sports days attracted more girls to join. Women were only appointed to leadership of these groups after being interviewed to be sure that they truly loved the Lord, knew Him personally as Saviour, had a good grasp of the Scriptures and knew how to present biblical truth in a way that girls would be drawn through them into an assurance of personal salvation.

During the first 60 years of its existence over 150 Classes were opened, with a total membership of over 5,000 girls. A Bible Correspondence Course (Lones) had 2,000 girls actively taking part, and 1,500 ex-Girl Crusaders had joined the Associate Fellowship as prayer partners, and over 700 girls had attended the Easter and summer camps. On average one ex-Girl Crusader every month had gone overseas to preach the gospel in a missionary capacity. The Union was thriving.

But in the 1970s and 1980s, like so many other Christian youth organisations, numbers were dropping. Groups were fewer and smaller, and it was proving harder to gain and keep Leaders. The Central Council, after much prayer, decided to launch a 'Forward Movement Year' to increase the public image of the GCU, to explain to the parents what the Union was seeking to do for their girls, to challenge each girl in every Group with their personal need of salvation, and to present a clear missionary challenge to all those girls who truly loved our Saviour. Would WEC lend me to them for that year? After prayerful consideration, the British home staff of WEC International agreed to this suggestion. Their Leader, Robert Mackey, led a dedication service in GCU Headquarters to launch this special effort. That same evening we had our first meeting, a seniors' supper with 30 senior girls from London Groups.

For me, the mental switch involved in changing from preparing material to present to university students, church congregations and women's meetings, to thinking in terms of schoolgirls – from 6-year-olds in primary schools to 18-year-olds, taking their final exams in secondary schools – was not exactly easy. Very little of the material I had used in the previous five years was applicable to this new task. Also the difference between speaking to a school assembly of 5 to 7 years olds, and seeking to communicate meaningfully with a roomful of 16 to 18 year olds, was enormous, far greater than the differences between the various groups in the previous tours. The Lord gave me a lovely bright yellow Fiat 127 for the year's work, and it became very well known all over the UK. Girls made maps, marking in all the GCU Groups in England, Scotland, Wales and Ireland and, using a small model of my yellow car, they followed my progress week by week. At the same time as this Forward Movement Year was launched, I was trying hard to complete the preparation of the manuscript of *Living Faith* for the publishers.

Two camps in the summer holidays, both in Scotland, with Bible studies and missionary challenge talks to the girls, and morning devotional talks to the Leadership, helped to get my mind attuned to the task ahead. That October we started in earnest, with forty meetings all over Scotland in the first month. Everywhere I was given such generous, loving hospitality by Leaders. Everywhere girls came and listened well in their various Group meetings. Every now and then a public meeting was arranged to introduce a wider audience to the work of the GCU, and to encourage other parents to send their girls to our weekly Groups. Three meetings were arranged on successive Monday evenings for 'Teens and Twenties' in the Glasgow area. Some sixty young folk came each time and seemed very receptive to a missionary challenge: the world we live in today in all its need; the God we love and worship in all His power to supply that need; ourselves, the means God graciously chooses to use to channel His supplies to meet that need.

Visual aids were definitely part of the plan of campaign. Several times, using the letters G – C – U – 'God' in His great grace on one side of the board, 'Us' in our sinful and selfish need and lost to His saving power, on the opposite side, and the 'Cross' of our Lord Jesus Christ, the only way to bridge the chasm between us and God, a chasm caused by our sin. As Isaiah says: '*Your iniquities have separated you from your God.*' At other times, I used a large flannelgraph presentation of our GCU badge, and built it up. The white background represented God's standard of holiness. The big red Cross reminded us of our Saviour Jesus, the only Name by which we can be saved, and the four small crosses spoke of our response to His saving grace – to say 'No' to all that displeases Him, and to say 'Yes' to all that pleases Him. Finally the golden border reminded us that our Lord and Saviour is now seated in heaven, preparing a place for us and praying for us.

I was invited to speak at the Scottish Scripture Union Camps' Reunion in the midst of that month, and someone helped me to paint a large flannel background depicting Mount Everest and the way that explorers attempted to climb to the top. Using the four letters C – O – S – T, we followed that pathway, from the base camp (the need of **C**onversion to start the upward journey), up the icefall to the advanced camp (by **O**bedience to the map, and to the instruction book, wearing all the correct gear such as goggles and crampons). Then we traced the long haul in the shadow of the mountains to the assault camp, be it by means of **S**acrifice or **S**ervice, even when the way seemed long and tedious, and when, at times, the final peak was hidden from view. And then, with our eyes on the goal, we looked at the last slog up to the summit, the wonderful **T**riumph when we finally reach the glory of the Lord's Presence. The responsiveness of those four hundred youngsters was so exciting, and that means of sharing God's challenge for wholehearted commitment to Him became a very popular presentation.

In Dundee we had the first of many subsequent weekends, from a Friday evening through to the Sunday afternoon. I used a flannelgraph of a lantern to illustrate the truth of Christian living. The frame of the lantern was used to point to our bodies in which Jesus wished to live. The wick, clean and long enough to carry the oil to the light, was used to portray our thoughts and minds. The glass, clean and without a crack, through which the light could shine, reminded us that our actions, our lifestyle, had to be consistent with our testimony. The oil that had to fill the lantern was a picture of the Holy Spirit with whom God fills us when we come to Him for forgiveness of our sins. And the LIGHT, being the Lord Jesus Himself, who comes into our lives when we open the door and invite Him in! Again, we were all humbled and awed at the gracious working of the Lord in the hearts of the thirty girls who were there that weekend.

There were special meetings, some for Leaders, others for parents or interested friends, and a number at church youth fellowships. Variety was the order of the day! With all the travelling involved, being available to chat to folk in the homes where I stayed, and writing letters before and after meetings, there was very little time for preparation of new material. I soon realised how essential it was to have time dedicated to such preparation between each section of the tour.

My work that year with GCU involved over 400 meetings and 24,000 miles of driving! I know it was very exhausting and yet, at the same time, strangely exhilarating. There were moments when things were far from easy. Some years previously, GCU had had another similar year with Miss Cicely Radley, a lovely, gracious lady, leading it. Reports of that year were impressive by their visible results. Many girls joined the Groups, several in all parts of the country signified that they had heard the call of the Lord in their hearts and responded to Him, and some women went forward willing to become Group Leaders. Somehow, it wasn't quite so obvious this time ... and I began to feel a failure. I knew perfectly well that we should not compare ourselves with others, and the results were all in God's hands, not ours. But nevertheless – perhaps particularly when weariness was the order of the day – I was caught in the snare. Then in the November, after a hectic four weeks in the London area followed by a time in south Wales, I heard that Pat's mother had to go into hospital for major surgery, just at the very time when Pat was moving home. And I wasn't there to help.

Someone who came to one of the open meetings told me after it that she had heard the same message a month before when she came to hear me in London. Did I only have one message? I nearly broke down and wept. 'What do they expect of me?' I cried out to God. There were two or three meetings every day, and in some places the same people turned up at several of these! Then I had a meeting with sixth-formers in a large girls' school, about 180 of them crowded into the room, and I had 35 minutes to speak to the subject, 'Can God really cope in the 20th Century?' followed by 40 minutes of animated discussion.

Yes! indeed Yes! God can cope in all situations, whatever the understood need. His power is the same today as it was 2,000 years ago when He worked such wonderful miracles in the days of Jesus Christ. And at that moment I sensed God's smile as He rebuked me for bothering to compare myself with another Christian worker, for questioning His timing about my not being at home when I felt I was needed there, and for reacting when someone indicated disapproval at hearing the same message twice. All that was necessary was that I knew I was in the centre of His will, seeking to please Him and trusting Him moment by moment. I had really no right to waste time feeling sorry for myself or getting angry with God. Had He not taught me several times in the past that it is all *privilege* to be invited by Him to have even a tiny part in His programme of reaching out to others?

There were many challenges during those months. One Group celebrated its 50th birthday, another was a get-together of GCU Associates who were all senior citizens. Then there was a special meeting for parents where one father told me, 'I wouldn't send them if they were boys!' From that I gathered that, although not a church-going person himself, he was scared for his two daughters in today's world and wanted us to give them moral standards that would protect them from all that would assail them in the years ahead.

Prayer days with Leaders were specially blessed to my heart. I often shared with them thoughts from a sermon we had heard in our own church on the word *'Philotimeomai'*, which apparently only appears three times in the New Testament, and which means 'Consider it an honour' (although often translated quite differently in our various modern English versions!). In 2 Corinthians 5:9 we read, '*we make it our goal to please him.*' In other words, if I realise what an honour it is that God condescends to be pleased with anything I do for Him, I will surely struggle to please Him at all times. Nothing will be too much trouble that is pleasing to Him. In 1 Thessalonians 4:11 '*Make it your ambition to ...*' Paul goes on to remind them of all he taught them about being Christ-like, about living lives that truly portray Jesus to others. If I realise that God allows me the inestimable honour of reflecting the loveliness of Jesus to others by living a Christ-like life, surely I will indeed study to portray Him more perfectly, more accurately? In Romans 15:20, we read: '*It has always been my ambition to preach the gospel where Christ was not known ...*' Should that not be my greatest desire, to strive to preach the gospel wherever the Lord sends me? If I realise what an honour it is to be entrusted with His precious gospel, I will leave no stone unturned to share Him with all whom I meet.

As we went through these thoughts together, with times of prayer between each, we asked God to make His Word alive in our hearts. These days it is so easy to have other ambitions and desires and motives than simply pleasing Him. How necessary it is to be willing to check out everything by this one standard – does it, will it, please God? Again, we were all very conscious that 'what you do speaks so loudly that we cannot hear what you say'. And we asked God to search deeply in our hearts and to reveal to us if there was anything in our daily lives that was spoiling the image of Jesus so that others could not see Him reflected in us. We earnestly wanted an ever-increasing willingness for the Spirit to '*conform us to the image of God's Son*', to sanctify us and make us clean mirrors of His glory. Thirdly, we looked at our willingness – or lack of it – to buy up every opportunity to preach the gospel. How easy it often was, when it came time for the weekly Group meeting, to feel 'Oh, no, I just don't want to go out to teach those girls!' or just to feel 'Can I not have one afternoon free to myself? Does it have to be *every* week?' And we asked God to deal with that part of our nature that shrank from total involvement in this task of preaching the gospel and teaching the girls committed to our care.

I always felt renewed and enabled to keep going after one of the days of prayer that were woven all through that year of ministry. How good of God to organise it in such a way! He knew my need, and He met it before I really became conscious of it.

It was back to Northern Ireland in December, for meetings that included a residential houseparty for some senior girls, two carol services and three meetings in Belfast with 'Teens and Twenties', and a Camps' Reunion, with ninety girls from all over the Province. Their excitement was infectious, and really was a rebuke to any feeling of weariness or wondering if what I was doing had any eternal value.

Just after Christmas there was a Union-wide Camps' Reunion in London with over 200 girls in attendance. That was marvellously exciting! Girls who had first met at the summer camps met up with each other and chatted away twenty to the dozen. All sorts of camp-like activities took place in different rooms: crafts, team-games, even sweet-making. Then there was a Bible study for each age group before a magnificent tea, which was followed by 'the Challenge'. The talk, based on the word 'F - O - R – W- A – R -D', was illustrated by an enormous painting of a £100 note. I actually had a £100 note in my hand – a red note that the Northern Bank graciously 'lent' me in exchange for ten £10 notes that I 'lent' to them! On one side of the giant imitation note we attached the letters F, O and R in turn – and we reminded ourselves of all we had learned in our Groups and at camps throughout the past year: Forgiveness of sins, if we confess and trust in the blood of Calvary; how we must be Obedient to all God's commands that we read in the Bible, to show Him that we love Him; and how we can Rejoice in hope, knowing we are saved and kept by His Spirit. It was summed up in the phrase 'Christ died FOR us.'

Then we turned the huge note round and attached the letters W, A and R. We are saved to do WAR against the devil and all his wiles, to overcome all his subtle temptations, and to stand up for Jesus 'no matter what'. We are to **W**itness with our lips; we are to be **A**pproved workmen, acting as Christians every day; and we are to **R**each out to others, telling them about our Saviour. In fact, we are to '**WAR** a good warfare!'

Having looked at each letter in turn, and thought about where each one of us was in our own Christian lives, we realised that God was challenging us to go forward with Him. We held the note up, while a helper shone a light through from behind it, and the girls saw a large **D** in the 'blank' watermark space. D was for 'Now then, **D**O it!' (1 Chron. 28:10,20) was our final challenge, that we should go out into our everyday lives – at school, at home, when studying, when playing, wherever – and live for Jesus, seeking to 'please Him' in all the little details of life, as well as in the great big decisions that have to be made. That was our message to the girls and to us.

In the weeks that followed, letters came in from Leaders of many of the Groups in different parts of the country, from Tiverton in Devon, from Cardiff in Wales, from Harrogate in the north of England, and from Groups around the London area. All these shared with us conversations they had had with their girls during the journey home about what they had enjoyed most about their day in London. Many shared how the Lord had spoken to them personally, and how they really wanted, by His enabling, to go **forward** in their Christian lives, asking the Lord to help them every day to be pleasing to Him. Our hearts were thrilled by God's gracious goodness to us in allowing us just a glimpse of what He was doing in girls' hearts. And that certainly gave me fresh courage to keep going into the new year.

Another Leaders' Quiet Day for those in the London area re-awakened in all of us a deep desire to go forward with God, to grow in grace and in knowledge of our Lord and Saviour Jesus Christ, and in an ever-increasing determination to be available to serve Him every day of our lives. We looked at the principles underlying revival in Scripture, concentrating on a passage in 2 Chronicles, from the close of chapter 28, where King Ahaz shut up the house of God and turned to the worship of foreign idols, into chapter 29, when Hezekiah *'did what was right in the eyes of the Lord'*. During sixteen days he cleansed the temple, carrying out all the accumulated filth that had gathered, then re-established the sacrificial services. And in chapter 30 he gathered everyone together to 'return' and to 'submit themselves to the Lord their God.' We read *'The Israelites who were present in Jerusalem celebrated the feast .. with great rejoicing!'* By the close of that day we all sensed a renewal in our hearts and spirits, and an increased hunger and thirst to be pleasing to our God.

After a month of meetings in and around London and the Home Counties, the tour took me to the south coast, to Lansdowne, Ferndown, Wentworth and Bournemouth. Several school assemblies brought a new challenge. We compared ourselves to civil servants, who can use the letters O-H-M-S (On Her Majesty's Service) on their letters instead of stamps. Only, as Christians, the letters stand for 'On **His** Majesty's Service.' We are called into the high profession of being God's civil servants, willing to be sent anywhere at any time, willing to do any job our Sovereign Lord King asks of us, and always knowing, without a shadow of doubt, that He will be wholly responsible for us – not just for stamps on the envelope! It was such a joy to share with them stories from my twenty years of missionary service in Congo, to illustrate how wonderfully I had proved this true in my own experience. He never fails us. He is always there, and always able, whatever the need.

From the south coast, I travelled up to the Midlands of England, and another Leaders' Quiet Day. We worked our way through the three chapters of the prophet Joel, seeing the exceptionally severe plague of locusts, wave after wave, in chapter one, as a picture of all the wickedness of our day. We thought of laws that encourage immorality, lack of discipline in schools, industrial unrest, those who proclaim a post-Christian era and that God is dead, the insidious attitude of 'what do I get out of it?' that pervades everything, the ceaseless demands for 'my rights' – until eventually nothing is left, anarchy rules and the soul withers away.

But this terrible picture is immediately followed by a call to repentance. Should the condition of our world not drive us to our knees? There is no other way out. A devastating fire in the midst of overwhelming drought had destroyed any possibility of recovery. They were surrounded by unutterable devastation. This led to a trumpet call to WAR against sin, to repentance and to believing prayer.

Chapter two brought us to see the forebodings of the prophet. He saw the invasion of the locusts as a forecast of the anarchy of the last days. There is the inevitability of doom, the irresistible force of destruction as we read the prophet's description of the mighty army drawn up against them. Then in verse 11, the startling phrase: '*The Lord thunders!*' reminds us that He, and He alone, is at the head of the army at the last day. And the Lord's plea to us: '*Return to me with all your heart!* ' He wants us to plead with those around us, in His Name, as His ambassadors. '*Rend your hearts! Repent! Return to the Lord!* ' God challenged us. Were we awake to the awful responsibility laid on us to warn the girls committed to our care? A holy God must judge all sin and condemn all that is not according to His will. Dare we be silent? Once again, there follows a trumpet call to worship in repentance.

In our third session together we looked at the Lord's answer, and how precious are His promises! They are as real for us today as they were in the days of Joel. God's power had been doubted, His honour impugned, and His people reproached. Is it not the same today? Some say that God is dead! Others insist that God can't cope! And on television they make a joke of anyone portrayed as a minister. In Joel's day God was jealous for His great Name's sake. He *had to* intervene, and He will yet intervene today. He promises complete and total relief from starvation, ridicule and oppression, and all with the wonderful purpose '*Then you will know that I am .. the Lord your God!*' (2:27).

There follows an even more wonderful promise of not only material blessings, but also spiritual blessings. We must repent and be transformed, made conformable to the mind and will of God. He promised a great wave of spiritual revival. This began at Pentecost, at the birth of the church, and will find its fulfilment in that great and dreadful Day of the Lord '… *when everyone who calls on the name of the Lord will be saved!*' (2:32). I believe we all prayed that day with renewed earnestness for the lost, the mockers and the rejecters. We prayed that we would be found available to God, more than ever before, available to be His ambassadors to all those to whom He sends us, to warn them and pray for them.

I travelled on from there to Sheffield, Leeds, Harrogate and Bridlington. There were some tremendous meetings: youth rallies and school assemblies as well as church services. Each one was important; each one was different. Then I went over to Dublin, to a packed week, before returning home for a week to prepare for a hurried trip over to Canada for a weekend women's convention that had been arranged before the GCU tour was planned.

That took me to the final straight of this marathon. Throughout June I was to re-visit every place to which I had been during the year, and the GCU leadership was to organise 'rallies' in central places, where we could, by God's enabling, bring the challenges given throughout the many smaller meetings, to a head. Our prayer was that girls would come to the place of commitment, and step out with the Lord into a life of obedience. We started in Belfast then went across to Scotland where we held meetings in Dundee and Glasgow before travelling south to York and Sheffield. The title was 'At the Crossroads'. One GCU Leader's husband had made us a superb visual aid – traffic lights, that actually worked! **Stop** – and listen to what God wants to say to you. **Caution** – there are so many dangers and pitfalls if you don't obey. **Go** – go forward with your hand in God's hand, trusting Him and His Word, obeying Him and enjoying Him, and the Lord will go with you every step of the way.

It was a tremendous month with eighteen rallies in all, and we wept many times as we saw the Lord at work in girls' hearts and lives. The final thanksgiving service in London at the end of June was a most humbling yet uplifting time, as together the leadership worshipped our Lord and Saviour and gave all glory to Him for anything that had been achieved during the year.

Chapter Seven

Digging Ditches in the Slough of Despond

Living Faith was published in 1980, and appeared to be well received. I needed to begin thinking seriously about the preparation of *Living Holiness*. There was only one important public commitment in the immediate pipeline, as I had been invited back to Urbana, to the Student Triennial Missionary Conference in Central North America in December 1981. The title for the whole conference was 'Let every tongue confess that Jesus Christ is Lord', and Eric Alexander was to lead the four Bible studies. As in 1976, the conference sought to challenge the 17,000 young students who would gather there for their Christmas holidays, with the *needs* of the 3,000 million still unreached people in our world, and with the fact of our *privilege*, as well as our responsibility to be available to God to meet that need. The theme of my particular talk was to be 'The Spirit's Enablement'. That seemed to fit well with the slowly forming thoughts about the next book on holiness.

But there were other matters of more immediate concern, matters that were distressing me. During three months at home in the autumn of 1981, I became assailed by feelings of failure, of doubts, of insecurity. It was probably incomprehensible to others. I looked like a very self-confident, capable sort of person. In the world's eyes I was what others would have called 'successful'. But serious doubts began to assail me. Was I in the centre of God's will? Why was I not back on the mission field when I knew how urgently doctors were needed, when I had the language already and understood a good deal of the culture and the thinking patterns of those in Congo? Was it *my* choice to be in a fairly cushy job, where there was no danger, no real sense of sacrifice, in which I was always treated with a red carpet, looked up to, even sought after? Alongside all this, there was a nagging fear of being a failure. Did I really represent WEC? Why did my prayer life not match up to the desperate world needs with which I sought to challenge others? And at moments, especially after a tour of meetings, I could almost lose the assurance of my salvation. Was it only head knowledge and not heart experience? Verses such as: '*so that after I have preached to others, I myself will not be disqualified for the prize*' (1 Cor. 9:27) nagged at me.

I had written in my Christmas prayer letter (1981/82) 'I am enjoying the privilege of a year to "*come apart for a while*", to be quiet with the Lord'. I was living at home, seeking to be a normal member of a family and of our local church, writing hundreds of letters as a ministry instead of merely as a necessity, studying and praying without specifically preparing messages for public meetings and without deadlines. WEC had both counselled me, and agreed with me, that it would be wise to take on no more public engagements until September of 1982, when they, at WEC headquarters, would co-ordinate my programme, thus helping me to avoid the over-booking that had tended to overwhelm me during the previous three or four years.

But underneath all that, mostly unknown to WEC or others, there was turmoil in my heart. I simply could not share my deep heartaches with anyone. I tried once, but felt immediately that the person to whom I wanted to unload recoiled and drew away from me. Then I nearly panicked. So many people seemed to look up to me and respect me as a strong Christian, but if they knew the tempestuous battle raging inside my heart, would I hurt them? Would it shake their faith?

There were moments when it was so dark; I felt such a load of depression. I almost feared I was going to have a complete nervous breakdown. It was probably the result of what is commonly called burn-out (nervous exhaustion) from keeping up what some people thought was an unreasonable pace for so long. But knowing that did not help me to handle the problem. Sometimes it was like a crippling nightmare. Nevertheless, in the midst of it all, I *knew* that God *was* there, and that He *was* in control. I *had* to learn to trust Him utterly, to rest in Him and to cease from my own struggling. Besides everything else, I was suffering nightmares, re-living the horrors of the civil uprising in Congo, even though it was by then almost twenty years distant. I cried out to God for His mercy, for His deliverance. A small group of people prayed for me every evening, and one of the things they prayed for was that the Lord would give me calm sleep.

Then God seemed to say to me, 'Are you not willing?' And I sensed He was saying, 'This is a small price to pay if others are blessed by your testimony, if others are brought to see that I can preserve them in the midst of war and harassment and brutality. You have to re-live the experience as you speak of it or others will not sense the reality of all that occurred. And the greatest thing that occurred to you was that you had My peace in your heart even in the midst of the storm!' So was I not willing to suffer the nightmares? Was it perhaps, for me, the *'thorn in the flesh'* that Paul had prayed three times to have removed before God told him to accept it, not to pray to be delivered from it, and to receive the deep truth of that wonderful promise: *'My grace is sufficient for you, for my power is made perfect in weakness'* (2 Cor. 12:7-9)?

Through all of this, I was also struggling to know what God would have me share at Urbana. I was led to Judges 7, to the wonderful story of how Gideon was chosen by God to lead the people of Israel against the hosts of Midian, and of how God chose and equipped His chosen crack regiment to go against the forces of evil. The *subject* of the Urbana convention was, surely, each individual student as a potential missionary in the hands and the purpose of God. The *object* was undoubtedly those people in the world, estimated at that time to be 3,125 million, still in total ignorance of the Saviour. There had to be a *verb*, and obviously that could only be the indwelling of the Holy Spirit, making it possible for the subject to relate to the object. The subject, each one of us, needed to be a clean vessel, filled with the Spirit of Christ. '*We have this treasure in jars of clay to show that this all-surpassing power is from God and not from us*' (2 Cor. 4:7). But if the vessel, filled with the water of life, stays at home, how can it satisfy the thirst of a dying world?

Not only that, but as I looked more carefully at how God equipped His army, I saw *empty clay jars* covering smoking flax, and trumpets to terrify the scared enemy. The clay jar was there simply in order to be smashed so that the flax would flare up as a beacon of light. As we allow God to smash us (our ambitions, our selfishness, our pride, our rights) the Light can stream out to a needy world. As the woman in Mark 14 smashed the alabaster jar of very expensive perfume and the fragrance filled the whole house, was I willing (am I still willing?) to be smashed – utterly poured out, nothing held back – that others may be blessed?

How can anyone say 'Yes!' to such a demand? Our 'yes' is only by the indwelling Holy Spirit. He alone is the enabler. He is indeed the Spirit of Christ, who was Himself the first and greatest of all missionaries. Jesus left His Father's glory to come from heaven to earth in order to die. He made Himself of no reputation, even becoming a slave. He put obedience to His Father's will before everything else. Was He not indeed a perfect *clay jar*, willing to be smashed that I might live?

'Am I willing to be like-minded?' I had to ask myself – to give up my rights, e.g. to be married, to have a family, or a job, or security, to let go of my reputation and to become wholly submissive to my heavenly Father's will? Would I actually be willing to die if that would enable God to reach dying men and women with the gospel? How could I ever reach such a standard?

I could do it only as I asked the Holy Spirit to create such an attitude within me, making me 'like-minded to Christ'. He, the Holy Spirit was, and is, willing to move heaven and earth on my behalf to conform me to the image of God's holy Son, so that others will see only Christ in me, and not me myself. But without doubt, this has to involve a death to self. For years I have called this 'the crossed-out I life' of Galatians 2:20. '*I* (the ME who lives in me) *have been crucified with Christ and I no longer live, but Christ lives in me.*' Like the smashed clay jar in the Old Testament, or the smashed alabaster box in the New Testament, the contents – the light, the fragrance – could then stream out to the world in need.

When addressing the students at Urbana that year I touched briefly on the appalling need of the two thirds of our world out beyond the furthest reach of all missionary endeavour, still waiting to hear, for the very first time, the Name of Jesus. Then we looked at what seemed to me to be even more shattering than the plight of those millions, the apparent apathy of the Christian Church. I talked about the need of every missionary-sending agency for men and women sold out for God, in an abandonment of love '*to serve him without counting the cost, or seeking for any reward, save that of knowing that we do his will*' that was so overwhelmingly apparent.

But again, I asked, who can possibly give such devoted service? Only someone indwelt and ruled by the Holy Spirit of God can do that. He, who was the *verb* of the conference, the third Person of the Trinity, can enable the clay jar to be willing to go, and to carry, and ultimately to be smashed in order to release the Treasure to those in need. It was easy to identify with the thousands of young hearts who were questioning, 'Is it I, Lord? Are you really calling me to go? How can I be sure?' We thought briefly of the faith needed by the twelve apostles when the Lord Jesus gave each of them half of a bread roll and told them to go to the waiting multitudes and feed them. The bread only started to multiply after the apostles began to obey! God didn't fail them.

His grace was sufficient for the need. Five thousand were fully fed and many basketfuls of leftovers gathered up.

I testified to how the Lord kept us in peace during five months of captivity in the hands of ruthless and unpredictable guerrilla soldiers. And my God is their God. He kept me; He can and will keep them as they step out in obedience. One aspect of the wonderful ministry of the indwelling Holy Spirit is to transform us into the image of Jesus, and to make us '*more-than-conquerors*' (Rom. 8:28-39). He can enable each and every Christian to accept every detail of our lives from the hands of a loving Father with thanksgiving (Phil. 4:6), even in the face of suffering, misunderstandings, frustrations and even in the face of death.

I went home again from an astoundingly wonderful convention, with many students making a public response to the challenge, only to find that nothing had changed for me. In fact, things were worse. I now *felt* – oh, that verb again! – I felt a hypocrite. Those 17,000 young people were willing to be challenged by God to full-time missionary involvement, no matter what the cost, through *my* testimony, and here I was in distress, crying out to God to meet me at the point of my need. I even feared that I might not really be saved. At times Pat must have been so aggravated by me; I was so stupid! God had just blessed in an enormous way. Who did I think I was? Did I really think I could have influenced that vast crowd in my own strength? Of course it was all of God, so why did I question whether I was saved or not?

But this reasoning, however reasonable, did not help me. I really could not explain myself to myself or to anyone else. It was just a deep inner unrest and fear, a sort of emptiness, a sense that I had lost touch with God. I still read my Bible every day. I tried to pray, but I felt (!) that my prayers were helpless. I taught every week at a mid-week women's Bible class at our church and I taught a group of schoolgirls every Sunday afternoon in our GCU Group. I said the right words – I was even sure that they were the right words – but they did not reach through into my own heart. *'What a wretched man I am!'* Paul cried: *'Who will rescue me from this body of death?'* That is what I felt like crying out. I was desperate for a deep, meaningful encounter with God. I taught assurance to others; I knew the right Scriptures to quote. But when I said the same Scriptures to myself, they did not bring me the comfort I yearned for.

As I turned my mind to preparing the manuscript of *Living Holiness*, I was absolutely sure that God's standard for each one of His children was that they should be holy *'as He is'* (1 Pet. 1:15-16). Equally, I knew that I myself had not reached that standard. Yet the Bible clearly states: *'Without holiness no one will see the Lord'* (Heb. 12:14). With all my heart I wanted to see the Lord. How could I attain to that standard of holiness? It wasn't only then, as I sought to prepare to write a book on holiness, that this hunger took hold in my heart. No, I remember clearly, how many years before, at Nebobongo, when faced by an outbreak of smallpox, isolated in my home for several weeks of quarantine, I first read Bishop J.C.Ryle's book *Holiness*. It captured my imagination and filled me with a great longing, a hunger after true holiness. Holiness was surely what God planned to work in each one of us by the transforming grace of the Holy Spirit, making us into the image of His dear Son. This ongoing ministry of the Spirit would doubtless take a lifetime to bring to any sort of fulfilment.

Then, as I continued to pray over the subject, I realised that at times of revival the Spirit achieves that ministry in a person's life almost overnight – the life-long process appearing to be speeded up. If I studied the work of the Spirit during some of the mighty revivals in church history might I see a pattern of what the Holy Spirit desires to do in each of our lives? I acquired every book I could that recorded revivals during the past 150 years in Canada, Scotland, Ireland, Wales and the Congo, from 1854, through 1904, to the 1920s and on to 1954. I read and re-read the records until a certain pattern began to emerge. Each of the accounts of revival started with an overwhelming conviction of sin leading to godly repentance. As each convicted and forgiven sinner came to realise more fully what Christ had done for him at Calvary the love of God flooded over him, filling his heart with an intense desire to learn more of his Saviour through the study of the Scriptures. This in turn led on to an ever-increasing desire to obey every command that was written in Scripture so leading to godly lives, lives lived in an attempt to tell God how much His people love Him. And through that conscious obedience to the Word, came a wonderful willingness to serve others. Jesus, when He washed His disciples' feet, told them to serve each other as He had served them. Humility and the willingness to serve at all times, without asking, 'What do I get out of it?' became the hallmark of holiness.

These seemed to me to be four steps in the transforming work of the Spirit in our hearts, making us *holy as he is*: conviction of sin, overwhelming love, meaningful obedience and humble service. They do not necessarily come in that order. At some stages in life's journey one or other takes on the more important role, and it is not always easy to know where one ends and the next begins. In fact, I saw these four steps as the steps of a galloping horse. All four are essential. The horse will limp or fall if it tries to gallop with only three legs, but it is often well nigh impossible to see the order in which its legs move. So it is with the quiet, steady, inner work of the Spirit in each Christian life bringing us to holiness. Yet, even as my mind was grasping these thoughts, my emotions remained in turmoil. At times I felt a lonely coldness, as though I had altogether lost touch with the Lord. How could I pull myself out of my 'slough of despond'?

By the following September, I was back on the road again. I had several meetings in the Inverness area of Scotland before going to Switzerland for a month filled with over forty meetings, mostly spoken through an interpreter. What joy it was to be amidst the fantastic beauty of that land, from Lausanne and the lakes of the west, to Interlaken in the Bernese Alps, to wake in the early mornings to see the sun touching the JungFrau with a rosy hue, to enjoy the sound of sheep-bells, and see the myriad of tiny flowers in the meadows. What an extraordinary month that was! Everyone was so kind to me, so welcoming, so encouraging. Then I returned to the UK and another forty meetings in universities and Bible colleges throughout the length of the land. Once again, God graciously poured out blessing. Yet still the unrest in my own spirit remained. I read my Bible daily. I prayed. I prepared talks and sought to be pleasing to God. But the peace and the joy of such service were not there.

As mentioned earlier, in 1983 I went again to Australia. One of the themes during that two-month tour was 'God is at work in His world.' Using a large traffic sign that warned motorists of road works ahead, I commented on how frustrating these signs can be when traffic is brought almost to a standstill and there is no sign of any workmen or any activity! Does God want to put up His sign 'Road works ahead' in many countries all over the world, but is hindered from doing so because there are no workmen available to Him?

At the final houseparty the leader asked a group of some twenty of us to be available at the close of each meeting to counsel any who stayed behind afterwards. I was very nervous of this, as I did not feel that I was in a sufficiently positive Christian state myself to be able to counsel anyone else, but I acquiesced to his request. At the end of the main meeting that morning a number of people stayed in their seats after others had left. We sat quietly waiting. Then the leader asked me to go to a lady halfway down the marquee. I went and knelt beside her, and waited. The lady was sobbing, and obviously in distress. 'Can I help you?' I asked quietly. She turned to me with such a blank look, almost of agony and helplessness. 'I am the wife of a pastor,' she sobbed, 'but I have lost my assurance of salvation!' Then she poured out such a sad story of past usefulness and blessing compared to present emptiness and failure, and all seemed to hinge on one word, 'I don't *feel* ...' As she shared with me, it just seemed as though she was describing exactly where I had been for the past year or so. 'Can you help me?' she pleaded.

'I think I can!' I almost laughed. It was suddenly all so clear. I remembered when I was first saved, hearing teaching at a CSSM beach mission, using a simple flannelgraph representation of a train with an engine, a tender and a coach. They were labelled Fact, Faith and Feelings. The train came to a sharp bend in the tracks and Feelings fell off. Feelings nearly pulled Faith off, but Fact puffed on, strong and unaffected. The *fact* of our salvation is unshakeable. Christ died on the cross of Calvary for our sins. If I confess my sins, God is faithful and just to forgive me my sins, and to cleanse me from all unrighteousness.

Together we looked up these verses (1 Cor. 15:3, 1 John 1:8-9) putting our fingers on them in the Bible, and there was the *fact* of our salvation. Yes, we acted in *faith* when we first came to believe these wonderful truths for ourselves, but that faith had not saved us. The fact of Christ's death saved us. And even if our faith failed, that could not alter the fact of Calvary. As for *feelings*, they come and go, they fluctuate; they do not stay the same two days running. Feelings are quite unreliable as an index as to whether I am saved or not.

'Yes,' she said, 'I can see all that, but ... God no longer speaks to me. I am not able to feed on His Word as I used to.' And the Lord brought into my memory a simple story I heard somewhere, likening our heavenly Father to a gardener. He had three women working in His garden. During the day, He came into the garden to see them at work. He passed by the first woman, saying nothing. He stayed a short while with the second, encouraging her to keep on. Then He spent a long time with the third, sitting down and talking gently to her. The following day almost the same thing occurred. At last, the first woman could not contain her distress any longer. 'Why do You not stop and talk with me?' And the Lord smiled at her, 'But I know your love for Me. I do not need to comfort and help you as I do the other two!'

Even as I shared this with that dear woman, I was conscious of the Lord smiling at me, and saying, 'Are you listening?' The comfort wherewith I sought to comfort another had turned back to me, and I was comforted! That evening, I *knew* that God had put into my heart the reassurance that I had *felt* I lacked. I knew all was well. The doubts were an attack of Satan to seek to stop me in the ministry the Lord had entrusted to me. My longing to *feel* good, to *feel* saved, to *feel* needed, was to be exchanged for a deep realisation of His unspoken love, His outpoured grace. I cannot say that the doubts have never sought to assail me again, nor that I have never become distressed by lack of feelings, but I do know with quiet assurance that His peace in my heart is due to the *fact* of Christ's death for me and has nothing to do with my *feelings*. I prayed earnestly for that dear woman, that she too might have found release from the enemy's attack and a new joy in her service for the Master, a joy unrelated to her feelings.

It was shortly afterwards that the Lord had to speak to me again along similar lines. I had been eight years in this roving ministry, living out of a suitcase, travelling all over the English- and French-speaking worlds, challenging men, women and young people to put Jesus first in their lives, to trust Him utterly, and to move out into a life of obedience to Him in every detail. But still deep in my heart was the niggling doubt as to whether this was really what God had chosen for me, or if it was merely an opt-out of my own creating? Should I be responding to the challenge and go back to Congo to serve as a medical missionary again?

I had the opportunity to go to Portstewart in Northern Ireland to the annual 'Keswick Convention' there, staying in a caravan with a lovely Christian lady companion. And I pled with God to meet with me during that week, and to speak to me so clearly that this problem could be finally dealt with. Just before the first evening meeting, I met a young friend in the car park, a missionary on her first home assignment. She was having a problem knowing, with complete assurance, whether God wanted her to remain in the UK to care for her ageing parents or go back to the mission field for a second term of service. I spoke to her briefly, assuring her that should she need to talk and pray over her problem with anyone, I would consider it a privilege to be available to her. But I tried to make it very low key, as I certainly didn't want to butt in where I was not wanted.

By the Thursday evening I was just yearning for God to speak to me. My own problem was as big as ever – to stay here or to go there? Please, please, God, speak to me clearly, I yearned. And I sensed that it would be that night that God would meet with me in a definite way. As we drew into the car park for the evening meeting, there was my young friend. 'I need your help, please!' she said. And I shrank. Dear God, please not tonight. You were going to speak to me at this meeting! But, as I had offered to be available, we got into my car and I drove us out to a parking lot on the headland looking out on the Atlantic Ocean.

After making us each a cup of coffee, I asked my friend how I could help. She poured out all the tussle that was going on in her heart, the apparent pros and cons on both sides of the problem, and the heart cry to hear a word from God giving her clear, unmistakable guidance. 'When you first went out to the mission field, did God give you a verse of Scripture to stand on?' I asked. Yes, indeed He had, and she shared with me how the Lord had guided her so clearly. We went over this two or three times, from different angles, to re-assure her of the clearness of her original guidance.

'Let us look at Isaiah 30:21: *Whether you turn to the right or the left, your ears will hear a voice behind you saying, 'This is the way: walk in it!'* When will you hear a voice re-directing you into the right way?' I asked. 'Only when you turn *out of the way,* turning to right or left! But if you remain *in* the way, the Voice does not have to speak again. God has not rescinded the calling He gave you; He has not pointed you in a new direction so He does not need to give you another word!' Immediately my friend was filled with joy and with a consciousness of the peace of God. She just knew, without a shadow of doubt, that God had spoken to her.

Having driven her home to where she was staying, I returned to our caravan annoyed with God. I had been so sure that He was going to speak to me, to meet my urgent need of guidance, that very evening. But the evening meeting was now almost over, and I had neither reassurance nor peace. I lay on my bed, got out my Daily Light, and argued with God. 'Why have You not spoken to *me*? You have given my friend peace and joy, why not *me*?' As I read Daily Light, it was as though God said to me, 'I have spoken to you, but you are not listening.' I read the words again. 'God, You say You have spoken to me, but I have not heard. Please, speak again!' Then I was brought into a state of conviction. 'Do you think that you were speaking to your young friend out of your own cleverness, out of your own mental deductions? Surely, I was speaking to her through you. She listened but you didn't!'

I went back over all our conversation together that evening and suddenly my heart was filled with light. Yes, God had clearly given me a word from Himself in 1972, telling me to prepare to leave Congo in order to go home to the UK to nurse my dear mother. WEC, my Mission, had agreed when I shared this with them. I came home from Africa to the UK, and was with my mother for two years. Then Mother died, somewhat unexpectedly, although all our family knew how fragile her hold on life had become. Thereafter I was asked to do deputation work for the Mission, nine months of it in USA, before – as I thought – returning to Africa. During that time I became unwell and needed surgery to remove a malignant cancerous tumour. While I convalesced, I was asked to continue doing as much deputation work as I reasonably could. Asking God for a clear word of direction at that juncture, he said: *'Make this valley full of ditches.'* Again, I knew it was God's voice, and accepted this word as His direction for my immediate future.

Since which, through eight years of deputation travelling and speaking, daily 'digging ditches' (many of which God graciously filled with water, blessing many young people), I kept on asking Him for another word, for further direction. Could I not trust what He had already said? Was I mistaken? Had He not meant what I had clearly understood Him to mean when He spoke to me through 2 Kings 3:16?

That evening God spoke to my missionary colleague through what Isaiah wrote in 30:21. He reminded her that if we turn out of the way of His will, either to the right or to the left, we will hear a voice behind us, prompting us to come back into the way of His will. We had together concluded that the corollary of that was that if we *are* in the centre of God's will, we will not hear the voice, as we will not need re-directing, or called back into the right way. Was I listening? I had heard God's voice, and passed His message on to my friend who had heard, listened, accepted and received with joy the Word of God to her heart. But was *I* listening? Apparently not! As I lay on my bed in the caravan that evening, God spoke right into my heart, and I *knew* – at last – that I *was* where He wanted me to be, doing what He wanted me to do. Why had I taken so long to heed God's Word?

More recently I have been corresponding with a dear young friend who, six years ago, was in a terrible accident which left him a helpless paraplegic, in a wheel chair, totally dependent on the help of his wife and others, frequently in pain, and distraught with the frustration of the whole situation. I have kept all our emails to each other over the past four years. His latest heart cry reads, 'I am literally totally in the dark. My prayer life and my heart for Jesus seem to continue to dry up. I don't think that I am being a hypocrite but feel that to pray, confess His truths ... is done in the flesh. ... I feel that my grace period has ended because it has been going on for six years, and I'm beginning to get some of Job's friends' responses (when I broach the subject with other people)...'

I have just written back to this dear sufferer, and I believe my reply may well have been born out of this chapter. For that reason I reproduce it here. 'You spoke of your "dark night of the soul" experience ... your whole world turned upside down ... and all the past (knowing who you were and what you were supposed to be) has been stripped away, "and I don't know what I am supposed to do or be." Let's start there. Basis: God is in charge and in total control. Nothing can touch you except He allows it. And He only touches you with the tenderness of touching the apple of His eye. For a time in our Christian lives we 'go along', growing, developing, knowing who and what we are ... and then God sees that we are ready for a radical and total change. We may have begun to rely on who we are and what we do ... and God says, 'No! Rely wholly and only on Me.' So He appears to strip away all the props, all the known things, all the known and accepted 'feelings' that go along with our Christianity. It seems dark – even frightening – insecure – what's the point? And God is wooing us into Himself, independent of everything else. We have to put our hand in His in the darkness, seeing nothing, possibly even understanding nothing – but simply trusting. He cannot do us harm. He will never hurt us pointlessly. But if He strips us of all we know, all we hold dear, all that is certain, it is because He wants us to be wholly His. He is a jealous God. He will not share our love and service and worship with another. And if He sees that even a tiny scrap of self-pleasing has crept into my service, if He knows that I am beginning to rely on my being able to do what He wants me to do, and not wholly on His being able to do what He wants done even when I cannot ... then He must strip me of myself, of my dependence on my ability, even of my apparent ability to know Him, and share Him with others.

'Does all that sound like nonsense? Yet in my heart it is making sense to me. As He strips away all of myself, and my self-reliance, He is actually making me into the clay jar He wants to indwell. He is ridding me of anything and everything that He sees could hinder the free flow of the Holy Spirit to others. I was just reading Acts 8 an hour ago, preparing Bible study notes for our little group at church, and seeing how He (the Holy Spirit) ordered Philip away from the region where he was being mightily used, possibly at a time of revival, and leading him into a desert place ... a lonely road ... to meet one lonely African eunuch, probably a proselyte to the Jewish faith, but still basically a despised foreigner, on the fringe of temple worship because of being a eunuch. But God, who had set the scene, took Philip into it, and he was able to buy up the opportunity and preach Jesus!

'Going back to your letter – you have said, 'It's one thing not to know His purposes for my life, but quite another matter not to know what He wants of me.' No, no! That is the next step in the darkness. We do not have to know anything except that He is El-Shaddai – He is the great Almighty Creator God who loves me and loves you, and in some amazing way, who has chosen us to be part of His programme. He does NOT have to explain to us how or when or in what way. We just HAVE to rest in Him, in unquestioning trust. Let Him have YOU, all of you, all your thought processes, all your desperate desire to understand, to know the meaning of this whole protracted process. Stop hankering to know what He is not choosing to explain to you yet. Oh, how relatively easy to write that, but how infinitely harder to put it into practice. Give over to Him the impatience; give over to Him the longing for the joy and peace of the past. Just let Him be the ALL for you in the present.

'You say, "I beg the Lord to heal me or let me know if paralysis is to be my life." Then you say He doesn't answer you. He does, dear, but you are perhaps not entirely willing yet to hear His gentle whisper ... and possibly others keep on feeding other desires, which contradict God's gentle answer. I sense that He does not wish to heal you – He could, and if you press Him hard enough, He yet may – but I sense that is not His highest will for you. Psalm 106:15 (KJV) is frightening: *He gave them their request, but sent leanness into their souls.'* Take your hands off. You feel that all is virtually lifeless now ... no! That is not so. It is just that the life has gone down to a deeper level. It is real LIFE, life in Him, life that is no longer dependent on feelings, or seeing answers to prayer, or knowing that you are being used etc. You say, "I long for a personal relationship, but there seems to be no-one there." Oh, but He is right there! His love surrounds you, upholds you, envelopes you – but it is FACT, not feelings. In that glorious day when we shall see Him face to face, and we shall weep at His beauty, He will at that instant fill us with an amazingly sweet knowledge of Himself, and a deep quiet shattering realisation that, Yes! He had been just there all the time!

'Dare I lovingly challenge you, are you hanging on to the desire to be healed? You have asked Him for His best for you, and if He knows that this pathway through the darkness is overwhelmingly more wonderful than mere physical healing, can we together embrace that and accept that we must go at His pace? ... We dare not race ahead of Him, nor lag behind. Yes, dear, you (and I) are seeking to pray for others, to serve others – we long to be light and life to a dark and needy world – but do we want to do this in our own chosen way, in a way that seems to make sense to us? Can we trust Him to do it through us, even when it seems to make no sense?

'I read on through your letter – being like John the Baptist... and the disciples when others all left Jesus ... and then you go on to liken yourself to Job (even though you don't actually name him) when you say, "I despise the day I was born." Job at the end of his testimony came to accept the almighty greatness of God as the most real thing in his life, despite all the circumstances, and he realised that we simply cannot understand the mind of the Almighty with our little puny human minds. But we can accept. Accept His will. Accept His way and His plan. Even accept the dryness, and the sense of loneliness, lostness. Do you remember when the Brook Cherith dried up? Elijah was where God told him to go, doing what God told him to do; yet the Brook dried up. And God knew that it would dry up! It didn't dry up because of any sin in Elijah, or any failure of obedience. Not at all! It was just part of God's perfect plan. When Jesus told the disciples to cross over the lake (Mark 4:35), He knew that the furious squall was going to blow up, and that they wouldn't be able to cope. And it wasn't because of anything they had done wrong. It was part of the fulfilment of the will of God (Mark 4:40,41). Is that where we feel we are? Terrified! But Jesus was there in the boat with them. And He is in your boat and mine, and He will never leave you or me alone.

'I do not know if anything I have said – or could say – will actually help you, but I just pray that God will break into your thought processes and help you simply to say "I accept!" no matter what.

'Jesus is able, and He is the ONLY ONE in whom to trust. There is no other way, no other god, no other Name given among men in whom we must trust for our salvation. May He fold His arms around you and give you His peace – even if you don't feel it!'

And what I wrote to my young friend, I seek to apply to myself.

Chapter Eight

Digging Ditches Hither and Thither

In the summer of 1983 I was invited to speak at a conference in Eastern USA, at what I understood to be an American 'Keswick Convention', a week of biblical teaching on spiritual holiness and our individual responsibility to walk with God in our daily lives. The Ben Lippen property was partly owned by Columbia Bible College, and partly by the Billy Graham Organisation. I felt honoured to be asked to take part, and expected to speak at one meeting, giving a challenge to full-time cross-cultural missionary service – in what we used to call the Missionary Day at Keswick Conventions. Arriving there two days before the Conference was due to start, I was flabbergasted to learn that I was expected to speak each day of the week, giving the daily Bible Readings as well as the Missionary Challenge. I had twenty-four hours in which to prepare!

It was an amazingly hot week. The sides of the marquee were rolled up, but as the air was so still this barely helped to reduce the temperature. Crowds came the week's convention, including a large contingent from Augusta, Georgia, with a number of medical consultants and students among them. I confess I felt overwhelmingly inadequate for the situation, not least because I had no messages prepared. Until then, my deputation ministry had been almost entirely 'one-off' missionary challenge meetings. Now I was invited to give a series of Bible studies with no specific mandate as to subject matter!

At that time I read right through the Bible in each year, and my daily reading that weekend was in Jonah. I was immediately reminded of my last months in Congo, some ten years previously, when the students of our Nurses' Training School accused me of mishandling college funds. That was a shattering experience. At that time (also in July) I was, once again, reading the Book of Jonah. God had spoken to me – eventually, when I was willing to listen to Him – on my third reading of the book! Subsequently, when at the WEC Missionary Training College in Tasmania, the students and I worked our way through the Book of Jonah, chapter by chapter, looking at the biblical principles of guidance, of prayer, of knowing and giving God's message to the people to whom we are sent, and of our own relationship with God and with His message. Unfortunately I did not have any notes with me of those meetings, but I sensed that that was to be the theme for the week's meetings.

I spent that Friday night before God on my knees at my bedside and with an open Bible before me. 'God's prepared Message', His Son, our lovely Lord Jesus, the One who died for our sins, who was buried and rose again on the third day for our justification, became once again the central pivot of all I longed to share. Oh, for the grace of God to so share Him with others that they would see His infinite beauty and indescribable worth!

Throughout the Sunday the Lord helped me to clarify my thoughts as I prayed my way through the message for each day of the next week, focussing on God's preparation of His messengers, using the phrases 'the Lord *prepared* a great wind and a violent storm' and 'the Lord *prepared* a great fish.' By implication 'the Lord had *prepared* a great city,' and 'the Lord *prepared* a weed, a worm and a scorching east wind.' To what wonderful lengths the Lord is willing to go to make us what He wants us to be! And how stubborn we can be, resisting the pressure of His loving hands, as He shapes and re-shapes the vessels He is making! I was so blessed in my own soul as I worked on the details of each talk, and thought through the Lord's abundant goodness to us each step of the way.

During the week I was asked to suggest a missionary project for their weekly love-offering. My heart was full of the urgent needs of our little hospital, deep in the forests of North east Zaire (as it then was, Democratic Republic of Congo today). They needed to replace all the mud-and-thatch buildings with permanent structures, to stock the pharmacy with medicines that could only be procured with hard currency from outside the country, and to fund bursaries for student nurses and medical auxiliaries. I had an album of photographs of the hospital, from our earliest buildings in 1953 up to the time of my last visit in 1973, with pictures of the teams of male nurses and girl midwives. Everyone was interested, and they asked many searching questions. At the Thursday devotional meeting a love-offering was taken up. On the Friday, they presented me with a cheque – I nearly fainted. It was in five figures. I had never, ever received such a gift before. I cried. I simply did not know how to express my gratitude to them all. I could just picture the faces of both missionaries and Africans at Nebobongo when they heard that people thousands of miles away from them cared so much as to pour out such a gift to help them. It was indeed overwhelming!

After the Friday evening meeting, and all the many goodbyes to such a lovely group of people, I remained at the Conference Centre over the weekend, in order not to have to travel on the Lord's Day. What I had not previously understood was that the Ben Lippen Centre ran several consecutive weeks of conference throughout the summer, and on the Saturday the next group arrived, as did the speaker. I had the joy and privilege of sitting in the meetings and being spiritually fed all day Sunday as a member of the congregation.

The speaker was none other than Richard Halverson, at that time the Chaplain of the United States Senate. He was such a godly gracious Christian gentleman and I was privileged to sit and talk with him on the Saturday. He gave me a signed copy of his newest book *The Timelessness of Jesus Christ.* Everything he said, everything we talked about, all centred on Jesus Christ and His great relevance to the needs of the world of our day. To hear him speak of Jesus Christ warmed my heart. Even in his very tone of voice there was a deep love for the Saviour. His life obviously revolved around Him. The Lord was totally central, pivotal to this godly man's existence.

At that time the second great Lausanne Conference of evangelical and missionary leaders had just taken place. There was great pressure, especially from third world countries, that missionary service should include social services, and not be restricted to the straight preaching and teaching of the Word of God. It became the starting point of a new phrase that stressed the importance of the need for a *holistic* approach in presenting the gospel. Warning lights flashed in my mind and heart. It was not that I disagreed with aid programmes and caring for the whole person, especially in crisis situations. But I feared that these would take over and squeeze out the ministry of the Word. I had known this battle during my twenty years of service in Congo as a doctor, where we were always surrounded by need. The never-ending lines of sick people needed care, and the work of the hospital filled almost every waking moment, but I was out there in Congo in order to point people to the Saviour. Was my main ministry being squeezed out of existence by the urgently needed humanitarian ministries? It was hard work to keep the priorities right. We strove to maintain the first hour of every day for Bible study together in the church building. Now it appeared possible that all missionaries were going to be pressurised to do more, not less, on the humanitarian front, and as a direct consequence they would have less time and energy to spend on the preaching and teaching of the Word of God.

As I talked with Richard Halverson, and possibly began to air this fear, he said something I have never forgotten, 'When there is an international disaster, all the isms (not just Christianity, but also the communists and the atheists, the secularists and the philanthropists) rush to help. But there is one job that only Christians can do, and that is point people to the Saviour they need. That is our unique privilege, to show people the way to Calvary, to repentance and forgiveness of sin, and the deep inner joy and peace of knowing salvation from the hands of a crucified Saviour.'

I have just read Halverson's book, looking for where he expressed what he and I discussed on that long-ago Saturday, and a discussion that confirmed in me the urgent importance of maintaining the preaching of the gospel as the priority in my life. When I came to the eighth chapter, entitled 'As I have, I give' based on the story of the healing of the crippled beggar at the Beautiful Gate of the Temple (Acts 3:1-11), I found what I was looking for. 'One of our problems is that we have many deliverers of good sermons, and few preachers of the gospel. In the final analysis, preaching of the gospel is what the church uniquely offers the world, and this is that which the world stands ultimately in need of. Let us not sacrifice the gospel for any other message, however relevant and practical it may seem to be, for in so doing we are giving the crippled beggar a coin, when we might raise him up to his feet to walk and leap and praise God!' I thank God for keeping me at Ben Lippen Conference Centre for those extra two days after my own time of ministry was completed, in order to meet and have fellowship with this wonderful man of God around the Word of God, refocusing my heart and mind on the task the Lord had commissioned me to undertake in His Name.

I returned home excited and with a new conviction of direction. Shortly afterwards, I had the privilege of two weeks of ministry at our WEC Conference Centre in Scotland, and in the second of those weeks we centred our thoughts on Jonah. I began to realise that my ministry was to change from one-off meetings to a more Bible teaching emphasis, with a series of meetings at one place, giving opportunity for a deeper approach to the biblical challenge to missionary service. That autumn I spent six weeks in Canada, travelling from Vancouver in the west right across to St John, New Brunswick in the east. Women Alive and WEC arranged the tour together. It included ten women's conferences, with three or four meetings at each, eight Bible colleges (we studied the Book of Jonah together at most of them!), and ten different churches, as well as several high school assemblies!

In each venue there was more than one meeting, and I certainly found the ministry more meaningful and probably more likely to produce long-lasting results in lives. However, once home in the United Kingdom, during the six weeks leading up to Christmas, it was back to the one-off ministry, a very tiring, rapidly moving, apparently less productive method of challenging young folk to full time commitment to serve the Master wherever He chose to send them. Then it was on to the United States again for eight weeks with over 100 specific meetings, not counting all the private talks, interviews and counselling sessions. There was no doubt in my mind that, humanly, I could not keep up the pace much longer, and yet God was blessing! Why did I grumble? Why was I not content to allow God to direct as He chose? What did it matter if I was tired and/or lonely? Was Jesus Himself not both tired and lonely when He lived on earth?

During that tour the Lord led me to put together some thoughts on 'Motivation to Mission.' I was so conscious that many of the talks and challenges I gave, particularly in Bible colleges throughout America, were not apparently having the impact on young lives that I longed to see. The overwhelming cry of all missions was for full time career men and women, sold out for Jesus, ready for whatever cost might be involved, prepared to go anywhere that God directed, no matter how dangerous or difficult. Yet despite a great number of people being engaged in deputation ministry the cry was still the same. Missionary societies were not receiving the candidates they longed for.

I usually presented young people with what I believed to be a vivid description of world need, using a countdown system to enlarge their vision and understanding of the **CONDITION** of millions of people in our world today. Over **ten** hundred million teenagers, largely in the great cities of the world, desperately need to hear the Good News of a Saviour who loves them, and can deliver them from the problems of loneliness, worthlessness, drink and drugs. **Nine** hundred million Muslims, many of them becoming increasingly fanatical, follow a fundamentalist agenda of shari'ah law, with a deep-dyed hatred of the Name of our Lord Jesus. **Eight** hundred million atheists, who claim to live in a post-Christian era, where they have no time for, nor need of, God or a Saviour, believe that Christians are living in cloud-cuckoo-land. **Seven** hundred million Roman Catholics, many of whom believe in the virgin birth of our Saviour, His sinless life, His death on the Cross, do not understand that they can know Him personally and have direct access to God by prayer in His Name. **Six** hundred million Hindus, with all the intricacies of the caste system and thousands of gods, have no power to live a godly moral upright life. **Five** hundred million Buddhists, seeking to live moral lives according to a strict code of ethics, are without the enabling power of the indwelling Spirit of God. **Four** hundred million Protestants, who should know the truth, so often live inconsistent lives, denying the very standards of the God in whom they claim to believe. **Three** hundred million isms represent all those who worship at the shrine of the occult and/or the black arts, as well as all the cults and sects that abound today in ever-increasing numbers. **Two** hundred million – a startling figure – of born-again, Bible-believing Christians, who have put their trust in the Lord Jesus Christ, often seem to be so indifferent to the plight of those outside their fold, doing almost nothing to propagate the spread of the gospel among the two-thirds of the world who have still never heard the gospel. And I concluded by holding up a large **ONE**, and asking 'Are you the ONE to whom God is speaking today, seeking to challenge you to go and become part of the fulfilment of His great commission to tell the gospel to people of every ethnic group?'

Having heard me politely enough, they thanked me for going and challenging them. But how many responded and actually moved out of their comfort zone to train and to go to another people group, another culture, another land, to preach and teach the Word of God? No, I came to realise that just knowing the actual condition of the world in its great need is apparently insufficient to move people to take action. What then would motivate them to go and act?

I thought about the **CONTENT** of the gospel. Surely as we meditate on all that God has done for us we must be moved with compassion to do something about those other sheep that Christ wants to bring into His fold? Our God so loved the world that He gave His only Son, so that by believing in Him, men should not perish but should have everlasting life (John 3:16). God is not willing that any should perish, but that all should come to repentance (2 Pet. 3:9). I had reminded young folk that there is no other Name given under heaven by which men can be saved, only the Name of Jesus. There is no other way, no other Name, no other method than by conviction and repentance of sin, by believing and acceptance of God's free gift of eternal life through the merits of the death of His Son at Calvary. I know that God is holy, altogether holy, and that He must therefore condemn sin. We are all sinners, and therefore deserve only judgment and eternal death. But by the grace of God, He offers us forgiveness and restoration into friendship with Himself. I love Cecil Frances Alexander's hymn, 'There is a green hill far away', in which she says:

> There was no other good enough,
> To pay the price of sin:
> He only could unlock the gate
> Of heaven and let us in.

Christ died for our sins. He is the only true, sufficient and satisfactory Substitute to take the death that I deserve, so that by accepting His death in my place I might receive His righteousness. *'Look, the Lamb of God, who takes away the sin of the world!'* (John 1:29).

And with all that certainty in my heart, I know equally well that those without Christ are lost, that they are going to a Christless eternity. The Bible gives us no right to believe anything else. As we read in Psalm 19 and in the first chapter of Paul's letter to the Romans, God has made it possible for all to know Him, so that men are without excuse who choose not to know Him. But knowing all this – the fact of man's lostness, God's outstretched hand of love in Grace, the availability of salvation to all men – young people still did little or nothing. However yearningly I presented them with, and reminded them of, these truths, by and large they simply did not respond to my appeals for action. Neither the knowledge of the world's condition, nor the knowledge of the content of the gospel was apparently sufficient to motivate them into action on behalf of the lost.

What else could I do? I sought to share with people the need to obey the specific **COMMAND of Christ** to us, as His disciples, to: *'go and make disciples of all nations, baptising them in the name of the Father and of the Son and of the Holy Spirit, and teaching them to obey everything...'* (Matt. 28:19-20) that Christ commanded us. This has been God's purpose for His Christian people since the beginning. God promised Abraham that if he would pack up and leave his home city of Ur of the Chaldeans, leaving all that he knew of culture and customs and language, to go to a place that God would show him, He would bless him, make him a great nation, and that all the families of the earth would be blessed through him.

Matthew 28:20 is a COMMAND, not a vague request! If Jesus Christ is Lord of my life, I have a 'must' placed upon me. It is no optional extra, no matter of choice. There comes an implicit urge in my heart, along with this explicit command to go to tell others the gospel. Jesus said: *'As the Father sent Me,*

I am sending you.' He was sent from heaven into the world of lost sinners. He came to seek and to save the lost. Jesus came to serve us, to be a slave for us, willing to die for us. That is the where, why and how of the Father sending the Son. And Jesus says that He is sending us in like manner. Will we then go? Yet once more I discovered that even this clear command was insufficient to actually move people to leave their comfort zone and go to wherever God would send them to reach the lost. What **will** motivate Christians to obey, to care, to go to the waiting millions? I asked myself over and over again.

As I prayed about this problem, and wondered just how to present the challenge in such a manner as to drive folk to respond in a positive way, I became convinced that it was only as *'we have the mind of Christ'* (1 Cor. 2:16). When God the Father sent His Son into the world, to be born the Babe at Bethlehem, to grow up into manhood among all the sin of this earth, Jesus came. He obeyed His Father. Jesus did only those things that His Father commanded Him. He spoke only the words that His Father put in His mouth. He sought only to be pleasing to His Father, and to fulfil His perfect will. At the close of His three years of ministry, after His death and resurrection, the Lord said to His disciples: *'As the Father has sent me, I am sending you.'*

As we have the mind of Christ, that is, the very **CHARACTER** of Christ, we shall do as He did, think as He thought, obey as He obeyed, submitting always to God's perfect will. In the Garden of Gethsemane Jesus prayed to His Father: *'Not my will, but yours be done'.* Is that my prayer every day of my life? Should it not be the prayer of all our hearts? Paul said we were to be like-minded to Christ, having the same attitude to life as He had, *'who ... made himself nothing, taking the very nature of a servant, being made in human likeness. And being found in appearance as a man, he humbled himself, and became obedient to death – even death on a cross'* (Phil. 2:5-8). Have I the very mind of Christ? Do I exhibit the very character of Jesus Christ in my everyday life? Can others, looking at me, see a true reflection of Jesus, as in a mirror?

The more I prayed about this, the more convinced I became that as the **character of Christ** takes possession of each one of us, then, and only then, the **command of Christ** *will* become the great priority in our daily lives. This, in turn, *will* make it possible for the **content of the gospel** to compel us into action to share Jesus with other people, even as the **condition of the world** *will* drive us to tears and to prayer.

I gave this series of thoughts on 'Motivation to Mission', based on 1 Corinthians 2:16, '*We have the mind of Christ*', at the WEC Public Rally, at the start of another tour of meetings in 1984, and the Mission staff were tremendously encouraging to me. They sensed God's hand upon the presentation that evening, and saw its effect as it challenged many young people to commit themselves to whatever God had in store for them. So this particular line of thought became one of the main messages in my ministry during the next two or three years. Somewhere along the line, Dave Howard, one of the main forces behind the Urbana Conference in those days, heard me give this particular challenge. The facts are that no amount of knowing the dire condition of the world and its desperate need of the gospel will, of itself, move believers to take action. Being deeply conscious of the content of the precious gospel that is entrusted to us to make known to all men is, sadly, insufficient, of itself, to drive us into action. Even concentrating on the direct command of the Lord Jesus to all of us who truly love Him and have put our whole trust in Him and in His sacrifice on Calvary, to go to all peoples, all ethnic groups, throughout the world and to proclaim the gospel to them, even this appears insufficient, of itself, to motivate to action. Christians are so gripped by a defensive mechanism to protect themselves from hurt that they just will not take the risk. What then will actually motivate us to obey our Lord and Master? What will motivate us to take seriously the fact that all men outside of Christ are lost and are going to a Christless eternity? What will cause us to weep over the frantic state of the world today, sliding ever more deeply into a morass of sinfulness and wickedness, deliberate godlessness, unbelief and error, calling black white, and mishandling the Word of God? Only as we are indwelt by the Holy Spirit, allowing Him to change us into the likeness of Christ, truly giving us the 'mind of Christ' that we might think as He thinks, love as He loves, weep as He weeps – only then will we be motivated to move out, as Christ left heaven to become flesh and dwell among us. Only then will we be willing to be spent and not count the cost.

Dave got in touch with me in 1986 and asked if I could go to the next conference, at Christmas 1987, and give this particular message there, to challenge the thousands of Christian young men and women in universities across America at that time. The main thrust of the Conference that year was to be on outreach ministries in urban districts, and God's concern for those in the great cities of the world. When I arrived at Urbana, I was amazed when Ajith Fernando stood to lead the four Bible studies, and opened up at the Book of Jonah! They were exciting studies, and showed so relevantly God's concern for Nineveh, the greatest city of that particular time, full of cruelty and wickedness, not at all unlike the great mega-cities of today.

Then four different speakers took us to different great cities of our world and clearly laid in front of us their appalling needs. Two or three of us followed with passionate pleas for the students to listen to God's voice, and to heed the yearning in His heart that none should perish, but that all should be called to repentance, and to make their response. There was a tremendous response. All over that huge auditorium, students stood. Some were in tears, others looked excited, and some seemed almost stunned. Everywhere there was a deep sense of doing business with God.

Chapter Nine

Digging Ditches – a Renewed Emphasis

In 1986, just ten years after the Lord clearly spoke to me through 2 Kings 3:16, '*Make this valley full of ditches*', I looked back to evaluate the passage of those years. The initial emphasis had been on '*this valley*'. My mother had just died, I had undergone radical surgery for cancer, WEC was not planning to send me back to Congo and the Missionary Training School where I was to teach for one year was about to close down. Everything had looked very bleak. It was truly a valley experience after the mountain top that, in hindsight, the previous twenty years of work in Congo had been.

Then, slowly, the emphasis changed to the '*ditches*' – not a Suez canal, but just small, possibly insignificant ditches, perhaps with no apparent reason, and often with no apparent result. Their digging might well involve blistered hands and a sore heart. So began ten years of deputation meetings all over the English-speaking world, some evangelistic and others more specifically missionary-orientated. Some were challenges to service within the ranks of WEC, but many were more generalised in nature. I also became more involved in ministry in my local home church, in various Bible teaching ministries and in sharing with lonely and hurting individuals. Three books were completed in the series on the 'Four Pillars' of WEC.

Now, though I knew that I did not need a new directive from the Lord, I was keen for a word of confirmation that I was still in the centre of His will for me. The ten years of continual travelling and public speaking had brought considerable physical weariness. Writing three books, in between journeys and ministries, had caused some mental weariness. A fairly large correspondence and a growing involvement in a counselling ministry, as well as the preparation for all the speaking engagements, resulted in quite a degree of spiritual weariness. Ten weeks of 'flu, followed by a minor slipped disc episode was almost the last straw.

Yet at the same time, four weeks of meetings in Finland followed by ten days in London were an exciting climax to the year. It seemed that so many were helped, challenged, stirred and/or encouraged through those meetings, as well as through some newspaper articles and television interviews in which I took part. I was deeply humbled at the Lord's graciousness to me. When attending our British WEC Staff meetings, where I was going to ask the Leadership to pray with me about the possibility of re-direction in my service, I was invited to speak at the morning devotional session before the day's business started.

'What shall I share, Lord?' And the word came clearly: 'Make this valley *full* of ditches!' 'But,' I remonstrated, 'they have heard that message over and over again from me!' 'You haven't finished yet,' the Lord said patiently. 'The valley is not yet full!' So I accepted the Lord's gentle push to keep going, digging more ditches. And during that week, it was suggested that I should write the story of the first 75 years of WEC as a 75th birthday present for the Mission for the next year, 1988.

That launched me into an amazing year of research. The three books I had just finished were all basically auto-biographical, and needed very little research other than reading books on the matter in hand, and discussing with others who had been present at certain occasions to check the accuracy of my memory. I mostly knew the subject matter at first-hand. This was different. I wrote to many missionaries all over the world, from all different age groups, to ask for incidents from their different fields of service. I collected all the magazines from the WEC archives: British,

American and Australian, from the earliest days until the present times. I unearthed every book that had been written by a member of the Mission from 1913 onwards. And I started to devour the information available.

At the same time I spoke at several meetings in Canada and Belfast, Finland and in the USA, that had been previously booked. And there was no let-up in my correspondence responsibilities. It was quite hard to make adequate time available, in reasonably large blocks, to do all the reading that needed to be done. But the research proved to be amazingly stimulating and exciting. I re-read all the early biographies of WEC men and women: C.T.Studd, Alfred Buxton, Edith Moules and others. I became immersed in the magazines. Letters and cassettes from all over the world arrived, telling anecdotes and stories of the early days. Soon I realised that I was going to have an enormous quantity of material to draw on for one short book, and that the problem was going to be what to leave out as much as what to put in!

I started scribbling. After two or three months, I felt the book beginning to take shape, though not, perhaps, as I had initially expected. What was evolving was very short chapters, two to three pages at most, one for each year of WEC's life story, just to highlight some special feature within each year. The whole book would probably be some 150 pages long. The title *Living Stones* became apparent, as it was a potted-history of the *people* who made up the story, each a stone in the construction of the whole building. As Peter says: '*You also, like living stones, are being built into a spiritual house, to be a holy priesthood, offering spiritual sacrifices acceptable to God through Jesus Christ*' (1 Pet. 2:5).

Then I saw another pattern emerging. The early years were all bringing to the fore the principle of *sacrifice* as the essential factor in missionary service. The next group of stories, following the death of C.T. Studd, the founder of the Mission, underlined by the principle of *faith*, that no meaningful missionary programme could be effective unless underpinned by faith. Looking forward, I could see that in the third period of time, from the mid 1950s onwards, *holiness* had to become the most important element. And I knew instinctively that from 1970s onwards the most stressed of our 'Four Pillars' was *fellowship*. The story started with one man, with a vision for one country, using one particular manner of service. As it unfolded, it became the story of nearly 2,000 men and women, and countless nationals, in over forty different countries, using every conceivable method of presenting the gospel.

I wrote a rough draft of the first ten chapters, plus an overview of the whole, and sent it to our WEC Publications Committee to see how its members would react. They were not happy, certainly not excited! Apparently this was not what they felt they wanted, or what the Mission needed. We wrote to and fro; we phoned each other, and eventually I travelled across from Belfast to London to discuss the matter face to face. I then met with the British Leaders and asked their help to sort the matter out. I felt I knew what God wanted me to do; the members of the Publications Committee knew what they wanted, and we seemed to be poles apart.

I had to travel to Canada for two weeks of meetings, and it was suggested that I let the matter lie until I returned. By then, another person had been approached to produce the special book for the 75th year of the WEC. I was hurt, probably more deeply hurt than I at first realised. I really couldn't even pray about the matter. I was hurt, and felt I had the right to be hurt. I didn't want to pray about it, as I feared God would speak to me about my attitude!

Over the years, I have said to others, 'When you feel hurt, stop and pray.' As I have already written 'hurt' means that self is very much alive, and striving to get back on the throne of my life. If Jesus really indwells me, I ought not to be hurt. I may well be grieved at the behaviour of others, or by certain events, but not hurt. Hurt is a symptom of self. If I let the Lord have His rightful place on the throne of my life, He will handle that which causes the hurt. Oh, yes, the Lord had clearly taught me this on more than one occasion. But here I was, caught up again in the same difficulty. It seems that it is almost easy to say these things to someone else, but I did not want to say them to myself. Even though I had learned their truth so clearly in the past, I now had to learn it all again for myself.

While I was in Canada, at a Women Alive Conference at Waterloo University, I shared with nearly 2,000 women our need as Christians to be holy, '*to be holy as he is*', to be clean instruments in God's hands, based on 2 Corinthians 4:7: '*We have this treasure in jars of clay, to show that this all-surpassing power is from God and not from us.*' We looked at the four thoughts that God put in my heart when writing the book *Living Holiness*: repentance, love, obedience and service, as three steps to *inward* holiness, in order to offer *outwardly* holy service to others. God blessed that message in a very marked way. I was humbled and awed at His gracious goodness.

Now, as I faced the hurt in my heart, I knew I needed to repent of it. I knew it came out of my pride. I felt I could cope with this new book in a God-honouring way, and I was not really willing for anyone else to tell me how to do it. I guess I was proud of having been asked to write it in the first place and I was so sure that God had given me the inspiration as to how to tackle it. Consequently, I wanted to prove I was right. What a mess! 'I' was certainly in charge of my thoughts by that stage. 'Helen, give in and let Me control this situation,' God said. It wasn't as easy as that. I had dug my heels in and I wasn't going to give in without a fight. 'Helen, you're fighting Me,' He said in my heart. Of course, I knew God was right, but I still wanted to prove my point.

I had various local meetings during the month of May, and then back to WEC Headquarters for our British Staff meetings. The Leaders discussed the whole matter with me again, and I agreed to leave the book on the back burner till the summer was over. I was going to Finland for the Lahti Conference of the Evangelical Church in early July, and needed time to prepare for a series of five Bible studies there. God was graciously giving me breathing space, time to step back and cool off. He is always so patient and kindly towards us when He knows that deep down in our hearts we honestly only want to please Him.

The conference in Finland was a wonderful encouragement. Again I was led to take 2 Corinthians 4:7: '*We have this treasure in jars of clay, to show that this all-surpassing power is from God and not from us*' as the basis for our thoughts. Using the well-known chorus, 'Spirit of the living God, fall afresh on me; break me, melt me, mould me, use me ...' and we added a fifth verb, 'smash me.' As I spoke the words, the Lord was working in my own heart. 'Listen to Me, Helen!' he said. Was I willing for Him to continue His gracious work in my life, to make me more like His holy Son, our Lord and Saviour Jesus Christ? Every part of me wanted to cry out, 'Yes! Yes, Lord. Please go on. Don't listen to me saying, "Stop! Stop! I've had all I can take." Please, God, remember only that I sincerely asked You to take my whole life in every part, and to fill me with Yourself, and to work on me until others could see only Jesus in me, and not me myself!'

Back home again, and faced with the incomplete manuscript and piles of books and magazines all over the floor of my study, I could not run away from the situation. 'Dear God, what are You trying to say to me? Please help me to understand!' 'Helen, for whom are you trying to write this book?' That seemed an easy question to answer. 'For WEC, Lord,' I told him. 'I just want to thank them for all they have been to me, and done for me, over the past forty years.' 'Then you are doomed to disaster,' came the loving response, clear as a bell in my heart. And it was accompanied by a sudden strange reminder of a scene from my candidate's days at the old WEC Headquarters in south-west London, near the old Crystal Palace. I had just started my six months, trial period for me to test the reality of my call to serve for the rest of my life in the ranks of WEC, in acceptance of their principles and practice, promising loyalty and obedience to those over me in the Lord, wherever I might be sent. It was, at the same time, a time for WEC to test me, as to whether they felt happy with the reality of my call, my willingness to submit to direction from the leadership, my physical, mental and spiritual health, my reaction when put under stress, my understanding of what full membership in the Mission would entail and my unquestioning support of their faith attitude for the supply of all needs.

The first job I was asked to do was to wash out and clean the floor in the girls' toilet area. I scrubbed and polished number one area, and had just moved to number two to do the same there, when someone came in to use number one. She had muddy shoes on, and the floor was still wet. When she left, I moved back to number one and re-cleaned it. At the same time, someone came into number two ... and so started a kind of ping pong action between the two areas! I was reduced to tears, and frightened of failing to complete the very first job I was allocated. I would be a failure! I wouldn't gain the coveted title 'missionary'!

My senior missionary came in and stood looking at me for a moment, then realised I was crying. 'Helen, what is wrong?' I explained the impossible situation, that I simply could not complete the cleaning process under the presenting circumstances. 'Helen, who are you cleaning these floors for?' she asked. 'For you!' I ejaculated. 'You sent me here!' 'Then Helen, you will never succeed. You should be cleaning them for the Lord's sake. And He saw the first time you scrubbed the floor. That,' she said, pointing to the new mud recently carried in on the shoes of one of the girls, '*that* is tomorrow's dirt!' I laughed at the memory! It was as clear in my mind as though it happened yesterday. And here was the Lord trying to teach me the same lesson again. Why was I so stubborn, so slow to learn? 'Do each task for Me, and let Me handle the problems that arise,' the Lord seemed to be saying.

Accepting that WEC was unlikely to publish this particular manuscript, but that God was encouraging me to complete its preparation, I started again into the work of writing the book, with renewed vigour, and actually with renewed joy. Every chapter was a challenge. All the reading proved to be so exciting.

It opened up vistas of the history of our Mission that I had known nothing about previously. In 1924, for example, there was the amazing story of Fenton Hall among the Guajajara Indians, and how he died seeking to reach them with the precious gospel and without a murmur of complaint against God. His last recorded letter ended with the scribbled words, 'Yes, I *will* rejoice, *rejoice* in the Lord and in the God of my salvation.' Then, in 1925, there was a letter received from Rolla Hoffman, an American missionary, who had just gained access to Herat in western Afghanistan, telling of the overwhelming need for more workers, not only for the desperate medical needs of thousands, but even more because of the shattering spiritual darkness of those same people, 'Come over and help us!'

Jock Purves was one of those who responded, and he wrote amazing letters describing trudging through mountain passes, traversing narrow ledges overlooking precipitous cliffs, wading through ice-cold rivers, until at over 15,000 feet high, he could look down into Baltistan, 'a land without Jesus Christ; a land whose people have not yet had the Bible translated for them; a land largely unknown and unexplored.' Jock could see the shattering need of Afghanistan, Tibet, Russian Turkestan, Central Mongolia, Nepal and Bhutan, all without a single missionary. 'Oh, it is shameful! Oh, Lord God, for Jesus' sake, send forth the labourers into the harvest! Millions of souls – and no reapers – not even sowers yet!'

There were so many thrilling stories of missionaries like Pat Symes, in 1928, who started the work in the Republic of Colombia, of Alec Thorne in Spanish Guinea and Sam Staniford, along with Fred Chapman in the Ivory Coast. All these pioneers endured opposition and persecution, yet there was always a note of triumph in their voices! There were stories of the opening up of so many home bases for the recruiting, training, preparing, equipping and sending out of reinforcements, and for the tremendous task of prayer support in every area, and of keeping the 'over-timers' supplied with prayer fuel month by month. Somehow, I guess, I had always taken these ministries for granted. They were in place and working relatively smoothly by the time I joined the Mission. Now I saw a little of the price that had been paid to establish the work.

Then I reached 1940 in my reading. For each new chapter I read carefully through all the material I had gathered about that particular year. I then went back and read it all again, asking the Lord to highlight what He wanted me to write about. Sometimes this was easy; sometimes it demanded a third reading to discover a wee jewel tucked away in a small, almost unnoticed paragraph at the bottom of a page! But that year 1940, the story was clear, it was the account of Bessie Fricker of Portuguese Guinea!

'Bessie, a fair blue-eyed scrap of humanity, used to forage around market stalls ... for damaged vegetables ... scrag ends of meat ... to feed six hungry mouths at home in London's East End,' I read. And then followed the story of her conversion, through four fantastic years of patient Bible teaching, her dogged determination through three years at Bible School, knowing she had been called to be a missionary, and eventually the account of her going out to Angola to begin to study Portuguese, for her eventual entry into Portuguese Guinea. She suffered endless setbacks and hindrances and fought a lonely battle against the 'hierarchy' who were sure a woman – a *mere* woman – with difficulties with the language, would never be able to deal with government papers and legal requirements. Despite all obstacles, she did go eventually!

Bessie wrote, 'I know that God can look after me, and will; all that matters is to do His will! I go alone – yet *not alone* – I go with Him!' As I read forward through the ensuing years, there came the slow, almost painfully slow, story of victories in that land, where there is now a national church with national church leaders and evangelists, all because one woman dared to believe God and obey Him.

There were stories of the start of various new ministries to help to preach the gospel to all peoples: the birth of the Christian

Literature Crusade, Radio Worldwide, the Gospel Broadsheet Ministry, the Leprosy and Medical Crusade and others. Then there was the tremendous research ministry of Leslie Brierley (husband of Bessie Fricker-that-was).

The 'book' was rapidly taking shape. The next problem was to find someone willing to publish it for me. Two friends read the first draft, and both encouraged me strongly to go ahead and not give up halfway. I got in touch with my editor, with the publishers who had accepted the manuscript of my previous three books. She asked to see the manuscript, but sounded very dubious over the phone. 'Mission history is not exactly popular reading!' she warned me.

I realised that publishers took a risk. They did not want 5,000 books sitting on shelves instead of selling. All Christian publishers were saying the same things, that people no longer read as in the past. To print an edition of less than 5,000 was not good economic sense, but to print that number and fail to sell them wasn't sense either! Could I assure them I could sell 5,000? I swallowed hard. I was sure I could sell 500, but 5,000? However, God had pressed me into writing this book for His Name's sake, so could I not trust Him? Yes, *I* could, but would the publishers accept that reasoning? They were hardheaded businessmen.

I travelled to London to meet my editor. We sat in a restaurant, not far from the BBC Headquarters, and drank endless cups of coffee while she toyed with the manuscript. I explained the structure – it was pretty obvious, but I had to say something to persuade her. She liked the idea of emphasising the four pillars and could see that it really was not history, in the ordinary sense of that word. She agreed that she had enjoyed what she had read and been stirred by it. But ... we always seemed to come back to a 'but'. She honestly doubted if she could persuade her bosses to publish the book. However, she took the draft manuscript with her, and I returned to WEC Headquarters, and eventually home, to start the job of polishing the script. This always takes me longer than writing it and I tend to get very impatient with the detailed working-over of every paragraph, every sentence and every phrase – to be sure the right word has been used, the right emphasis given, as well as acceptable grammar!

Then the letter came. 'No,' said my editor, 'I'm sorry but the publishers do not think they can take this on at this time.' I rang her. 'At this time,' I said, 'do you mean you might take it on at some other time?' 'Well no, not really. I warned you that a history of a missionary society is not exactly popular reading these days.' 'May I come back to you?' I asked. 'Yes, by all means.' I went by myself to pray over the whole affair.

'God, I really felt You wanted me to do this book. I have been conscious of Your help and encouragement over and over again as it has developed. You taught me to take my eyes off what others thought, and to keep them on You and what You want. I have tried to do that, and it has been exciting! God, I honestly believe that You have made this book such that many people, who haven't previously been so, may be excited for mission. Has it just to die now?'

What if I offered to underwrite the production of 5,000? I wondered. Would the publishers accept the other 5,000, to make a 10,000 print run? Could I actually do that? Eventually I rang my editor, and asked her, 'If I had someone underwrite 5,000 copies, would you accept and print 10,000?' She had no idea how to answer. This was outside her remit. 'But,' she said, 'there is a Board Meeting on right now. I will go and put this suggestion to them and see what they answer. I'll ring you back.' I prayed earnestly for the next hour. I only wanted to be in the centre of God's will. I did not want to push open a door if He wanted to close it. The phone rang. 'Helen?' 'Yes.' 'The Board want to know who this benefactor is?' Silence. 'Helen, is it you?' I just could not answer. 'Helen, the Board say they cannot allow you to do this. They will print 10,000, and together we will trust the Lord to sell them!' I cried. How good God is!

I worked flat out over the next two to three weeks to complete all the corrections and submit the final manuscript to the publisher, who was going to have the book ready for the start of the next year – our Mission's 75th anniversary year! I was asked to supply names and addresses of all outlets that I knew would promote sales. I wrote round to every bookseller that I had ever had dealings with and beat up all the support I could. The book, *Living Stones* came out, was distributed ... and sold! Before the year was out, we had a further 5,000 printed. Write-ups in almost all the Christian press were so encouraging. Letters came in from all sorts of people, telling how they had been encouraged and challenged. Several missionary societies wrote to say that they were also promoting it to their people. Yes, God was good.

Most importantly of all, there was no bad feeling between WEC and me. The Mission had not felt led to accept and print my book, as they had already accepted another manuscript for the 75th anniversary. God did not let me have any sense of self-vindication in the excellent sales of *Living Stones*. Rather, He showed me that His way was best. As a large publisher produced it, He had organised that it reached far more widely into the general Christian public than would have been possible if it had remained an in-house job. Really God rebuked me for my lack of faith in Him in those difficult early days of writing *Living Stones* and reminded me constantly that His way is always best, if only I will wait for Him to show what that way is instead of pressing on with my own ideas. The book that WEC themselves produced was truly blessed and used of God in our own ranks. Had God not moved me out of the way, that second book might not have been written!

During the last few months of that year, whilst the book was at the printers, I had another tour of meetings in the United States, and I was so much free-er and more relaxed, more able to rest in the Lord and to enjoy the ministry. Four studies at Bryan College, ministry at First Alliance Church in Atlanta, Georgia and then at Toccoa Falls Bible School allowed opportunities to begin to focus on the fourth pillar, *Living Fellowship*. Thoughts began to centre on the relationship between the Three Persons of the

Trinity, as our perfect example of true fellowship – submission, servanthood and a willingness to suffer – with three symbols from the life of our Lord Jesus Christ: the yoke of submission (Matt. 11:28-30), the towel of service (John 13:1-17) and the cup of suffering (Mark 10:38, 14:23 and 36). I was beginning to become excited at the thought of tackling this last book to illustrate our WEC pillars.

Chapter Ten

Digging Ditches and 'Mama Luka Comes Home!'

For twelve months during 1988 I was invited to tour through England, Scotland, Holland, Australia and Canada, specifically to challenge young people in university Christian Unions, youth groups, Bible colleges and churches with the urgent need of two-thirds of the world to hear the gospel of redeeming grace. I was to discuss with them what such a challenge entailed and how they could train for their part in the fulfilment of the Great Commission, and what a life-long commitment would involve. All the study and reading I had done in the previous year into the history of WEC, with its principles and practice, aims and vision, fired me up for this.

At the same time, my mind was just beginning to turn to the fourth book on the Four Pillars of WEC, this one on Living Fellowship. I started thinking about this as I wrote the final quarter of *Living Stones*. But I knew it was going to take me some time to develop those few thoughts into an understandable book on what biblical fellowship was honestly about, as a *principle* for Christian living rather than merely a *methodology* of working together in teams.

I had the privilege of leading a Quiet Day for prayer and personal reflection at the Birmingham Bible Institute. There were three sessions of Bible study, prayer and meditation, during which we thought about those three symbols in the life of our Lord. The first, in Matthew 11:28-30, '*Come to me, all you who are weary and burdened, and I will give you rest. Take my yoke upon you and learn from me, for I am gentle and humble in heart and you will find rest for your souls. For my yoke is easy and my burden is light.*' The **yoke** – that heavy, unwieldy, wooden bar that holds two oxen together when ploughing, looks like an instrument of torture rather than something that is light and brings rest, until we remember that unresisting compliance to the pressure of the yoke makes possible a sharing of the load that more than halves the weight involved. The ox suffers no pressure sore on its neck if it keeps in step with its partner and does not seek to turn to right or left. In other words, the yoke causes no pain when the ox works with it in quiet submission. So as we agree to be yoked to Christ – what an indescribable privilege! – submitting to Him in unquestioning obedience, He takes far more than half the load and guides us to plough a straight furrow.

The second symbol we turned to was the **towel** with which Jesus girded Himself when He stooped to wash His disciples' feet at the supper in the upper room (John 13). At the end of the practical lesson that He gave them, Jesus said: '*Do you understand what I have done for you?*' … '*You call me "Teacher" and "Lord," and rightly so, for that is what I am. Now that I, your Lord and Teacher, have washed your feet, you also should wash one another's feet*' (v14). We are to serve one another as He serves us. There was a job to be done. They all knew that there was no slave to wash their dusty smelly feet before they partook of the meal, but not one of them was prepared to take the necessary action until Jesus Himself rose and took the towel. He saw a job needing to be done and did it quietly. He didn't stop to discuss whether it might be beneath His dignity, or demeaning to His status. He took off His outer garment, twisted a towel around His waist, got down on His knees and went round the circle of men with a bowl of water, washing their feet. That was true service. Are we willing to serve one another like that, without discussing our merits or place on the social ladder, or what esteem we will gain by doing it? True service does not count the cost.

Our third symbol was the **cup.** In Mark 10, as Jesus and His disciples were on their way to Jerusalem, the Lord sought to prepare them for what He knew lay ahead, for his betrayal, condemnation, mocking, flogging and crucifixion. At that moment James and John seem to have butted in and asked to sit on the Lord's right and left hands in His glory! Jesus must have looked at them, both sadly at their inability to understand what He was saying, and compassionately in His willingness to help to prepare them for the immediate future. '*Can you drink the* **cup** *I drink or be baptised with the baptism I am baptised with?*' He asked them. Surely Jesus was thinking of the intense agony and suffering that lay ahead of Him, the cup that He was preparing to drink to its dregs on our behalf. Shortly afterwards, in Mark 14, during the course of that last meal together with His disciples, Jesus took the **cup**, gave thanks and offered it to them: '*This is my blood of the covenant,*' He said, and they all drank, thinking of it as a cup of fellowship. A few hours later, thrown on the ground in the Garden of Gethsemane, agonising in prayer, Jesus cried out to His heavenly Father: '*Father, everything is possible for you. Take this* **cup** *from me. Yet not what I will, but what you will.*' Again, the **cup** – but not the cup of fellowship, rather the terrifying cup of suffering – the cup that our Saviour drank in its entirety that we might be saved.

Those 'cups' are one and the same. Yes, it *is* the cup of fellowship, but it is *also* the cup of fellowshipping in His sufferings. Wasn't that Paul's amazing prayer, as he languished as a prisoner in Rome: '*I want to know Christ and the power of his resurrection and the* **fellowship of sharing in his sufferings,** *becoming like him in his death*'? Are we willing to pray such a prayer? Are we willing to actually desire to share in Christ's sufferings as He continues to suffer for millions in our world today who are still outside His Kingdom? Can I ask God to help me begin to feel, as Christ feels, for the lost, the unreached, and the hurting peoples of our world in all their need? Jesus feels for their need of physical and material goods, yes, but far above and beyond that, He feels for their need of the gospel.

That day at Birmingham Bible Institute was an immense blessing in my own life. The Lord spoke to us clearly through His word, through these three word-pictures – the yoke, the towel, the cup – and the realisation that these three are each part of the deep biblical meaning of 'Fellowship'. The three Persons of the Trinity are a tremendous portrayal of true fellowship, submitting to each other, serving each other, and each willing to suffer in order to bring about the wonderful plan of salvation.

Through that year this theme became more and more real in my heart. It seemed to meet me wherever I went, during a marvellous day with the Girl Leaders of the Young Life Movement in northern England and another at a Bible college in central England, during a tour of meetings in Australia and at our own Mission Conference Centre at Kilcreggan in Scotland, even as I travelled in Canada and North America the Lord spoke to me on that same theme. Each time He prompted me to share it with others, it seemed to develop and shine more brilliantly with an increasing radiance.

That May Bank Holiday I spent at High Leigh at our GCU Annual Leaders' Conference, and whilst there, I was asked if I would consider writing a small book for them, for *their* 75th anniversary year! My natural instinct was to say 'No!' I had just finished working on a similar book for WEC, and the thought of doing all that research again made me shrink. But I had been a member of GCU for forty years and they had all prayed for me so intently during the months of captivity in Congo, this was probably the least I could do to say 'Thank you!' for all their love and care and prayers. So I obtained from GCU Headquarters in London all the early magazines and annual reports, copies of ever so many letters, especially those written to our large missionary family.

At almost the same time, I received a letter from my friend, Crawford Telfer, a Christian young man who was devoting his life to making videos for missionary societies all over the world, to help them promote their need of more workers and of more prayer support. 'Would you ever consider going back to the Congo to make a film to promote "mission" on a broad background?' he asked. Letters, phone calls, prayer and discussions followed as I sought to enter into Crawford's vision of what he was seeking to do. Without much difficulty we all agreed to 'give it a go.' Crawford had previously made a short 20 minute video of an interview between Margaret Collingwood and me at her home in Bristol. Margaret was an experienced radio worker and interviewer, and Crawford invited her to accompany us to Congo to do this proposed one-hour video programme.

Preparations began in earnest. Tickets were booked for our flight to Nairobi from Heathrow. Arrangements were made for our stay in Nairobi, where we were to collect visas to enter Congo, and obtain permission to film there. Our flights to Bunia and on to Nyankunde and Nebobongo to do the filming were planned. All the vaccinations and immunisations, paper work, the gathering of needed finance, the packing of the minimum of clothing so that all our allowed weight could be given to the filming equipment, had to be seen to. Eventually we were ready to go.

It was to prove an extraordinary month for me, and for each of the others in our party of four. I had been away from Congo for fifteen years. Would everything have changed almost beyond recognition? Would I remember the language? Would I recognise my friends? All those years I had hankered to go back, but now that the opportunity had come I was afraid. Would it work? Would it expunge the longing to return, and give me a better acceptance of my present ministry, or would it just increase my desire to go back full-time? Would I be able to do what the team wanted – not to act, but to re-live the past – so that they could make the film they envisaged? There seemed to be 100 unknowns. I was deeply grateful for Margaret's supportive friendship as she sought to enter into all my apprehensions and fears, yet at the same time to give me the reassurance I needed that this really was part of God's programme.

Everything went according to plan from the moment we were enabled to put through all our grossly overweight equipment without being charged a penny! We were given such a warm welcome in Nairobi, and our applications for visas for Congo went through more smoothly that I had dared to hope. At last, we were on the final leg of the journey, from Nairobi, via Kampala, to Bunia. At the small airport at Bunia, faced by the official inspectors who were prepared to open every bag and case and to charge us as much as they could, suddenly there was the big smiling face of one of the Africans I worked with all those years before! He had heard on the grapevine that I was coming and came down to greet me. We were waved through without a case being opened! So to Nyankunde.

The shock of seeing over 1,000 people at the airstrip to greet us – all singing, all waving bright bunches of flowers – of being swept off my feet into a huge armchair on the back of a truck, and being driven slowly around the whole village, every path lined by cheering crowds, took my breath away. School children, workmen and their families, nursing students, were all there, and the warmth of their love overwhelmed me. We spent a week there. I was invited to speak every day to different groups – in French, Swahili and English – including at the opening ceremony for the new college year for the nursing students! I just never knew what would be next. We were feted continuously, taken out to meals in different homes every day. And somehow, between it all, we filmed. We had to remember that this part of the film was to be at the end of the final version, so I had to say, 'Like we saw at Nebobongo,' or some such phrase, from time to time, even though we hadn't yet been there! They filmed in the home, in the church, in the local village and in the College. At the end, we had to climb the local mountain for the final shot. I had never climbed it before, even when I lived there!

From Nyankunde we flew on to Nebobongo. We had to stop at Wamba for three or four hours while the filming crew were taken to Nebobongo ahead of me to prepare to film our arrival! Here again, in Wamba, a tremendous welcome awaited us. Everything in the village stopped. 'Mama Luka (my African name, from Luke, the physician in the Bible, and Mama, as they call every older woman) Mama Luka has come back!' went up the cry, and folk poured across to the pastor's home to see for themselves! I shook hands, smiled, hugged, greeted … I suppose several hundred people, plus a couple of hundred school children. And would I please speak to them from the Word of God? All through that month, I had to be ready every day for impromptu speeches and Bible messages.

Eventually it was time to fly on to Nebobongo. The whole family was down at the airstrip. I wept. The joy was almost more than I could cope with. One of my dearest friends, Mama Damaris, already in her late seventies, was the first to greet me. Deep love shone out of the eyes of her dear wrinkled face. My colleague John Mangadima was there, almost in tears at the sheer joy of reunion, as was my house lad, Benjamino, ready with a glass of cold water. He was always considerate of my slightest need. Tall Samuel was there, at the back of the crowd. 'Asobeinobambi!' I exclaimed. He beamed, 'Only you ever remember my real name!' The ranks of school children sang a special song that Yandibio, faithful schoolmaster for over thirty years, wrote to greet me. And, of course, it was accompanied by excited banging on the native drums! Yes, I cried. It was just so wonderful, more than anything I had dared to imagine. And my Swahili came back as though I had never been away. We seemed to pick up conversations just where we left off fifteen years before. I was home, and I knew it.

We then started an intensive week of filming, firstly at Nebobongo itself, in the hospital, outpatient clinics, my old home and down at the leprosy care centre. Later on, at Ibambi, we interviewed other missionaries and national pastors, and attended a packed Sunday service. There were probably 2-3,000 people crowded inside the building and another 1,000 sitting on the ground outside! Pastor Ndugu, dear saintly man, probably in his mid-eighties, interpreted for me as I shared the Word of God at the morning service. We visited the village of Adzangwe to see a rural dispensary in action – one of the 48 that had been opened up within a 50-mile radius of Nebobongo. It was thrilling, not only to see that the nationals were continuing all the work that I had some part in starting, but also to see how that work had been improved and grown.

One evening the crew wanted to film part of the harrowing story of what occurred in that very house 25 years before, when cruel guerrilla soldiers broke in during the night and I suffered brutally at their hands. I was not to be part of that bit of the film as the crew, out of kindness and consideration, felt it would be too much for me to cope with. I went to bed, actually in the back room of the house. But of course, I could hear them … and I relived that dreadful night. Suddenly something inside me snapped. I just couldn't bear any more. I rushed out to them, and they were all very distressed and felt guilty when they realised how it had upset me. But actually, it was God's hand of blessing. That 'snap' proved to be the final healing of the hurts of that long-ago night, hurts that I had not really realised were still there. But that night God enabled me to hand it all over to Him, and to cease to harbour even a grain of bitterness.

Eventually, after 16 hours of filming, Crawford knew he had all he needed to make the video. So Margaret and I left on a whistle-stop tour around all the other WEC/church outposts throughout the Northeastern province of Congo. Mission Aviation Fellowship (MAF) flew us everywhere, and the welcome poured upon us at each stop was unbelievable. At Malingwia we had three meetings in the day and, from the outset, we sensed in a peculiar way the presence of the Lord with us. A number of young men came forward to give their lives to full-time service for the Master. It was both moving and humbling. At one church, where we stopped unexpectedly, the people gathered round us in obvious distress. We had arrived at a critical moment in a church conference, where there had been a difference of opinion between leading men. They were in deadlock. Those dear people allowed us to minister in the Name of the Lord. And in a very precious way God poured in healing oil, and there was brokenness on all sides. We stopped in at another mission/church centre at Lubutu for re-fuelling and, once again, a crowd gathered down on the airstrip and there was opportunity for a quick word of encouragement. The missionary there, who is involved in translation work, said it was just the Lord's perfect timing. How gracious God was to us!

We flew on to Mulito – our most southerly visit – to an area where Maud Kells worked for years building up the church, Bible school, hospital, leprosy care and primary school work. Again, we were privileged to minister at the opening of a new care centre for leprosy patients, and in the evening to the whole church including the Bible School students. It was thrilling to see how the work had grown, and all that was being accomplished so far from outside help of any kind. And it was as we were flying back to Nebobongo that the Lord first began to speak to me about the possibility of writing this book. He even gave me the title – *Digging Ditches*!

It was time to go back to Nebobongo and Ibambi district for our last few days, and I was invited to meet with all the pastors gathered at Ibambi. We were quite a small group, and they ministered to me, encouraging me to stay true to the Word, with my eyes fixed on Jesus at all times. They reminded me of certain biblical truths, such as Romans 8:28: *'We know that in all things God works together for the good of those who love him, who have been called according to his purpose'*. They had no doubt that I loved our Lord Jesus, and that He had called me into my present ministry. Then they thanked me for having become a member of their church family, there in Congo, and for submitting to their church discipline through my twenty years amongst them.

They thanked me for 'treating them with the respect of a child for its parents', as well as for all the various ministries, medical, material and above all, spiritual.

Then the pastors asked me to kneel and they laid hands on me, prayed for me and committed me to the Lord 'and to the ministry amongst English-speaking people worldwide to which He has called you'. In effect, they said to me, 'Go as our missionary, from our church, to all churches everywhere, to preach the gospel and to tell people of the great need of the world to hear and respond to the gospel.' Suddenly, at that very moment, I was filled with an overwhelming sense of peace – deep inner peace – from God Himself. The doubts that had plagued me on and off for so many years, as to whether I was in the centre of His will or not, whether I ought to have returned full-time to Congo rather than accepting a new direction for ministry within WEC, whether my present 'job' was an easy cop-out compared to facing the demands of front line missionary service – suddenly all these fears were put to rest, at least temporarily! It was not that the Lord had not spoken clearly to me on this matter before; He had, as at the Portstewart Convention some ten years previously, but I had allowed the same doubts and fears to surface again. But at that moment, in the meeting with the pastors gathered at Ibambi, God again gave me His assurance that I was doing what He had chosen for me to do, and it was just so wonderful to realise that my African family knew it too. They did not begrudge me my present work. No, not at all! Rather they sent me back into it with their blessing, as 'their missionary'. My sending church was there in Congo and the rest of the English-speaking world was my mission field!

Our last days in Congo were filled with seeing people, encouraging them and catching up with their news, as well as Bible teaching and preaching on every possible occasion. It was as though they just could not have enough. Then a very sweet thing occurred, almost like 'the icing on the cake'. I had been slightly conscious that some of the ex-patriot missionary family had not been exactly as welcoming as we might have expected when we first arrived. I vaguely sensed that they were afraid of my obvious popularity with the Africans, though I could have told them that such popularity grows ten-fold after one has left! When I lived amongst them I was no more popular than anyone else. But there was just a fear in some hearts that, maybe, I had come to show them how the job ought to be done.

In the last two days before we left, three different groups/ households invited me to join them in their homes for coffee or for a meal, and at each they asked my forgiveness for any lack of warmth in their welcome when we first arrived. I was deeply touched by their honesty and willingness to put things right. We prayed together and wept together. And I think in each instance, we entered into a new and deeper relationship of oneness in our Lord Jesus.

Home again. The month had flown by. We had covered hundreds of miles, met with thousands of people and spoken at thirty three 'official' meetings, and ever so many unofficial ones! We brought back a fantastic number of photographs and completed sixteen hours of filming that had to be condensed into a one-hour video presentation of those wonderful twenty years of ministry in the hinterland of Congo.[1]

For most of the following six months I stayed at home, basically in order to get on with the manuscript of the book for GCU. But at the same time I hoped to become more part of my local church family. I had the privilege of weekly meetings with ten young people, firstly studying the Ten Commandments and their relevance for us today, then eight studies on biblical theology based on the Creed (as used in Anglican churches). And I also enjoyed leading a weekly Bible study (mostly for women) through John's Gospel. In the summer I went for ten days to Holland, to the WEC Missionary Training College, with a group of senior GCU girls, for a working holiday. We all enjoyed the

---

[1] 'Mama Luka comes home' – by Crawford Telfer and available from CTA, Christian Television Association, Wraxall, Bristol BS48 1PG, UK (email:- info@cta.uk.com)

challenge of scrubbing, polishing, varnishing furniture, cleaning windows and making new curtains, of turning out a garden shed and re-vamping it, and of clearing a patch of ground and preparing a new vegetable garden. Interspersed between all these activities we had time for visits to local beauty spots and tourist attractions, and seven Bible studies based on Mark 10:45: '... *even the Son of Man did not come to be served, but to* **serve,** *and to* **give** *his life as a ransom for many.'* We took as our motto, 'Serve and give' (rather than 'be served, and get')! It was a truly wonderful holiday and we all felt we had met with the Lord in a new and exciting way.

The need to concentrate on writing the book for GCU was becoming increasingly urgent as it had to be finished and in print for January 1990. It was quite exacting work. Writing autobiographical books does not demand too much research, only a good memory and God's wisdom to know what to leave out (quite as much as what to put in!). But writing a history of any organisation demands a great deal of researching of all available material, and then putting such material together in a way that others will be inclined to read it.

Over several months I had read and re-read all the available material. Now began the job of sorting, and planning the structure for the book. Letters had to be written to everyone to be mentioned in the book, gaining their permission, and asking each one to verify the accuracy of what I proposed to include. Meetings had to be arranged with the various people in the text – older retired Leaders, the new leadership and Headquarters' staff, camp-leaders and associate members – all needed to have the opportunity to check the accuracy of their particular input into this history. Suitable photographs had to be found and a title chosen. The cover for the book had to be decided. I really had little idea of all that is involved in producing a book! Until then, all I ever did was write the text and then others handled all the countless jobs involved in turning the manuscript into a printed and published book.

But at last *On Track* was ready! It was an exciting day when we saw it piled on the bookstall at the annual GCU business meeting, ready to be bought and, hopefully, to be given away as Christmas presents![2]

---

[2] 'On Track', available from GCU Headquarters, 31 Catherine Place, Westminster, London, SW1E 6EJ

Chapter Eleven

Digging Ditches in Various New Situations

For twelve months during 1991 I stayed, for the most part, at home and concentrated on writing *Living Fellowship*, and on becoming more fully part of my local church and of our local GCU fellowship. I certainly enjoyed the quieter pace, and having more time for Bible study and prayer. I remember taking a series of Bible studies with a group of ladies, associates of our GCU family in the Lisburn area, on the Tabernacle, using this to illustrate the keeping of our daily tryst with the Lord – our own personal times of worship – as well as of public worship in church fellowships.

Another line of thought had been developing in my heart. I woke very early one morning with a verse of Scripture imprinted in my mind. *'Then the fire of the Lord fell!'* (1 Kings 18:38). I lay there in the dark meditating on that verse and bringing back into my mind its context. The 'Then ...' at the start of the verse challenged me to think through what occurred before this verse to make possible the falling of the fire of the Lord. I lay quietly thinking of Elijah, the shepherd boy, who was probably brought up in a God-fearing home and taught much of what we can read today in the first five books of the Bible. Angry at the state of his world at that time, so far away from godliness and obedience to the Ten Commandments and living with idolatry and promiscuity on all sides, might he have challenged Jehovah with His own words? '*Be careful, or you will be enticed to turn away and worship other gods and bow down to them. Then the Lord's anger will burn against you, and he will shut the heavens so that it will not rain and the ground will yield no produce, and you will soon perish from the good land the Lord is giving you*' (Deut.11:16-17).

God, why don't You do something? Why don't You stop the rain as You said You would? And did God say, 'OK, Elijah. You go and tell King Ahab that that is what is going to happen?' And Elijah obeyed God and went. (1 Kings 17:1) In my mind, I thought through the next chapter, how Elijah fled from the anger of King Ahab and hid in the Kerith ravine where God fed him with meat brought daily by ravens. Then the brook dried up and God told him to go to Zarapheth to a widow lady. Elijah obeyed and went. There the widow lady took him in and cared for him until the end of the years of drought. Through all that time, Elijah was doubtless learning deep spiritual lessons from God, lessons of absolute dependence on God alone and not just on His blessings, but also about the importance of immediate, unquestioning obedience to the Word of God without demanding explanations, and about the ability of Almighty God to undertake and provide for and protect His servant, no matter what the situation.

God then sent him back to King Ahab to challenge him. Elijah obeyed and went, even though he may well have had fear in his heart. Did Ahab not hate him and blame him for all the ills and tribulations that had fallen on the people due to the three years of drought? There follows the remarkable story of chapter 18. Elijah told Ahab to summon all the people including all the prophets of Baal to meet on Mount Carmel for a public contest – 450 prophets of Baal versus Elijah, the prophet of the Most High God.

'*How long will you waver between two opinions?*' Elijah challenged them. '*If the Lord is God, follow him; but if Baal is God, follow him*' (1 Kings 18:21). Then Elijah called for two bulls to be brought, one for the prophets of Baal, one for himself. '*Let them cut it into pieces and put it on the wood but not set fire to it.*' The prophets of Baal were to call on the name of their god, and Elijah would call on the Name of the Lord. '*The God who answers by fire – He is God!*' After the prophets of Baal had done all this, and cried unavailingly to Baal for fire, Elijah had to act. This seemed to me to be the beginning of the conditions necessary for the fire of the Lord to fall. First he had to rebuild the broken down altar of God, then to kill the bull and cut it up ready for sacrifice. The wood had to be arranged on the altar, and after that he even demanded that the people pour on barrelfuls of water, until the whole sacrifice was soaking wet. Then he prayed and God answered with fire, fire that fell from heaven and burned up the sacrifice, the wood, the altar and all the water in the surrounding ditch!

Today we long to see God '*rend the heavens and come down*' in revival blessing, to answer by fire, burning up all the dross, all the selfishness, all the offered sacrifice, and convincing the people of His power and of His willingness to save those who turn to Him in repentance and with faith. What are the conditions that we possibly need to fulfil so that Almighty God may act? Surely we need to repair the broken down altars, to confess and repent of our own waywardness and our stubborn self-will, our lack of faith and prayerlessness, whatever and wherever we have allowed 'things' to come into our lives that seek to take over and displace our Lord Jesus from His rightful place as King.

Then we have to kill and cut up the sacrifices. We have to offer our '*bodies as living sacrifices, holy and pleasing to God*' (Rom. 12:1) – our very selves. We need to put our 'I' on the altar, our right to ourselves. Oh, that I would honestly seek to enter into Paul's wonderful statement: '*I have been crucified with Christ and I no longer live, but Christ lives in me*' (Gal. 2:20)! That requires death to self in all its forms: self-esteem, self-consciousness, self-justification, and our desire for a good self-image. Everything has to go that has to do with pride (where the middle letter is 'I'!), what I want, what I get out of it and always thinking that I know best. Jesus said: '*If anyone would come after me, he must deny himself, take up his cross daily and follow me*' (Luke 9:23). We need to deny our-SELF and enthrone Christ.

Why did Elijah demand that people pour water over the altar and the prepared sacrifice? Was it so that no-one could suspect him of cheating? He had not hidden some smouldering flax in the midst of the firewood, hoping for a change in direction of the wind in mid-afternoon to fan it into a blaze. The fire of God had to fall from above. It could not be worked up from below. It must be clearly seen by all to be *God's* fire, and not his. God demands absolute honesty and integrity; He will have nothing to do with guile or hypocrisy.

Elijah was so sure that God would indeed answer his prayer with fire from on high that he was willing to pile on the difficulties. Then he prayed – publicly – in a loud voice: '*O Lord, God of Abraham, Isaac and Israel, let it be known today that you are God in Israel ... Answer me, O Lord, answer me, so these people will know that you, O Lord, are God ...*' (1 Kings 18:36,37). There was nothing self-centred, nothing to justify or glorify himself in his prayer. And Elijah expected God to answer! '*Then the fire of the Lord fell!*'

In the years that have followed since that morning meditation, the Lord has led me to this passage many times, and always He has so graciously blessed me through it. God showed me that He had prepared Elijah through chapter 17 before He could trust him with the fantastic victory of chapter 18. Was I also willing for that continual preparation of heart and life that enables God to trust me to be His co-labourer in His vineyard? Do I allow God to train me daily to rely wholly on Him, and not on myself or even on His blessings?

But then the Lord led me on another step to look at the next chapter, 1 Kings 19. Here we see Elijah fleeing for his life, terrified by the angry Queen Jezebel. He told God he had had enough. All he wanted to do was die. I just felt I understood exactly where Elijah was! He was going through what I call 'the backlash'. After great spiritual blessing or victory, when humanly one would be expected to be over the moon and full of rejoicing, so often there comes an almost overwhelming sense of failure, of uselessness and even of depression.

The amazing thing is to realise that God understands this! God did not rebuke Elijah for this reaction, but rather He sent an angel to him to supply him with *'a cake of bread ... and a jar of water'*. Elijah needed a meal. After his continued journey to Mount Horeb, and a night spent in a cave, the Lord called him out into His presence, and spoke to him – not in the wind or the earthquake or the fire – but in a gentle whisper! How gracious and tender is our Almighty God! So God sent Elijah back again with a fresh commission and a fresh enabling to put that commission into practice.

God began to show me that chapter 19 was as much part of the preparation for the victory of chapter 18 as the events of chapter 17 had been. Before God was able to entrust to Elijah the huge victory that occurred on Mount Carmel, not only had He trained him in obedience and trust, but also God knew He could trust him to come through the backlash that would follow. I have found this a tremendous comfort myself. God did not prevent the backlash occurring, nor did He wait until Elijah was so perfected that no backlash would occur. No. God, who created us as humans, and therefore capable of reacting to the backlash after great events, does not condemn us for so reacting, but meets us at our point of need and provides us with *'a way out so that you can stand up under it'* (1 Cor. 10:13).

The following spring, I had the privilege of another ten days of ministry in the United States, starting at Nanibijou, a wonderful conference centre on the west of Lake Superior, down to Augusta, Georgia, in the southeast of the States. Sharing mostly from the almost completed manuscript of *Living Fellowship*, the Lord also led me into a fairly detailed study of Paul's second letter to young Timothy, possibly Paul's last letter from his prison cell in Rome. I enjoyed sharing this study with a most receptive congregation in a huge Presbyterian church in Knoxville, Tennessee, at their annual missions' conference. Each year at this conference the church ask the invited speaker to speak to encourage any missionaries there on home leave and also to challenge the congregation to consider their level of involvement in the world missions' programme – as those who give to support those who go, or as those who could go to swell the ranks of those proclaiming the gospel on the front lines, or as those who should get behind them in meaningful, regular, informed prayer. They gave me the overall title 'Fanning the flame!' from 2 Timothy 1:6, and that led me to study how Paul set about passing the torch on to young Timothy, and therefore how we should be seeking to pass the torch on to the next generation of younger Christians.

As we started out in 2 Timothy 1, we looked, firstly, at God's plan to meet man's need, a plan that involved a group of argumentative, vacillating disciples being sent to 'go and tell' the Good News to all peoples, to every ethnic group, without partiality or favour. There was no other plan. There was no other Name, given under heaven, by which men must be saved! The Lord Jesus is *the* way, not just one of many ways. And however frail and weak we may feel we have to be sure that God's Spirit of power, His Grace in the Lord Jesus, plus the sufficiency of the Scriptures are the divine resources that He gives to each of us, both to preserve His church and also to spread the gospel throughout the world.

Paul challenged Timothy (chapter 2) to be strong, to endure hardness, to strive and to labour so that God's plan to meet man's need might be met. This is equally true of each one of us today. God's power to meet man's need must surely be the indwelling Holy Spirit. It would seem possible that young Timothy was almost willing to throw in the sponge. It may have been in his nature to keep a low profile and to opt out of suffering. Maybe he was finding the whole task of mission too big to cope with. Then the aged Paul wrote him this letter to encourage him: '... *join* *me in suffering for the gospel, by the **power** of God!'* Paul didn't minimise the difficulties that Timothy would meet. In fact, he told him bluntly that any who would live as Jesus wanted them to would inevitably suffer and be persecuted. 'Keep going, son. I'm in the same boat, and I'm not ashamed of it!'

The God who has saved us, called us to be holy and sent us out to proclaim the gospel, has given us ***the*** Gift (not merely a gift!) of the indwelling Holy Spirit. The Spirit gave Paul zeal for the work even though he knew there was a price to be paid. Paul always had a goal in view, and he pled with Timothy not to drift but to trust God to keep him whatever sufferings might be involved. All he had to do was to commit himself wholly and unreservedly to Him. All God asks of us is to preach Jesus and to be unashamed of Him. He is our message; He is the Good News, *'the power of God for the salvation of everyone who believes'* (Rom. 1:16).

Paul challenges young Timothy, and so us, to be strong in the grace of Jesus Christ, enduring hardship as a good soldier, uninvolved in every type of self-indulgence and pleasing our Commanding Officer at all times. He challenges us to fulfil all the rules for entry into God's Olympics – intensive training, self-denial, no cutting corners – and therefore assures us of the victor's crown. And He challenges us to work hard and diligently even through disappointments, just as a farmer works with no days off but in the expectant joy of harvest. The servant of God must study hard to know the Word thoroughly so as to 'plough a straight furrow', not be drawn aside by distractions, and able to withstand all false teaching. We are to keep our eyes focused on our Saviour, the Lord Jesus Christ. In all things and at all times we are to be Christ-like in our actions and words, in our attitudes and motives. Just as He came *'to serve and to give'* so is that to be our sole purpose.

In chapter 3 of Paul's second letter to Timothy, we saw that the facts of the world in Timothy's day were just as they are today. The wicked seemed to be flourishing. But Paul continues:

'You, however,...' and reminds Timothy of his own testimony, and his one goal: *'to present everyone perfect in Christ.'* And what did Paul get for all he gave? The list is almost unbelievable. He suffered ill health, loneliness and misunderstandings. He was beaten, stoned, put in the stocks and had to endure false accusations. Most of us, faced with such a challenge, might well say, 'No-one in his right senses would choose **that!**' Yet Paul knew from the day he was saved on the road to Damascus what to expect. He knew that he would suffer in his service for God. Had not God shown *'him how much he will suffer for my name'* (Acts 9:16)? Are we prepared, in our day and generation, to so fall in love with Jesus that we are able to call all such suffering a **privilege**? We have to make the choice with our eyes open. Do we want riches here or hereafter? Then the living Word is liberated *'so that the man of God may be thoroughly equipped for every good work'* (2 Tim. 3:17) to which God longs to call us. We need be afraid of nothing except failing Him. He will never fail us!

And then finally in chapter 4:2, Paul charges Timothy, God's servant: *'Preach the Word!'* Study and stick to the Word. Everything else is secondary: '... *faith comes from hearing the message, and the message is heard through the word of Christ'* (Rom. 10:17). Paul warns Timothy – and so all of us involved in God's service – to keep his head! We must not be sidetracked or caught up in lesser issues, even in good things. The one job that only we can do is to preach the Word with endurance when mocked, with patience when all seems fruitless, and with love when we are criticised or ignored.

If we do this and stick at it our Lord and King promises the crown of righteousness. And what a triumphant ending to the letter! The elderly apostle Paul, in prison, waiting death, said: '... *so that through me the message might be fully proclaimed and all the Gentiles might hear it. ... The Lord will rescue me from every evil attack and will bring me safely to his heavenly Kingdom. To him be glory for ever and ever. Amen!'* (2 Tim. 4:18). What a wonderful encouragement for timid Timothy, and for all God's servants today everywhere in the world! All we are called upon to do in order to discharge our responsibility is to preach the Word, that the message might be proclaimed (2 Tim. 4:2) wherever God sends us and whatever the circumstances.

The following year, after sharing these thoughts in Knoxville, I had the wonderful opportunity of going to Poland to minister among the Campus Crusade for Christ workers from all over Eastern Europe. Once again we worked our way through these same four chapters of this last letter Paul wrote before his martyrdom. They grew on me and excited me. Each time I shared them the Lord showed me new things and new ways of presenting the truth.

Then, almost unexpectedly, the Lord led me in a new direction in ministry. I was invited to go to Hong Kong, and from there on to Singapore, to minister in our WEC home bases, and at churches and youth rallies, Bible schools and seminaries in their areas and to promote the whole concept of missions – that our God is a missionary God! It certainly was very exciting to see over 1,000 young Chinese Christians and, a week later, hundreds of Singaporeans almost sitting on the edge of their chairs listening eagerly to the challenge as though they had never heard it before.

That was the start of a specific ministry to visit and encourage our WEC personnel at many of our sending bases. I had already had this privilege in the USA and Canada as well as the UK, but now there were invitations to visit France, Switzerland, Germany and, a little later, Mexico! Each visit was interwoven with ministry arranged by and through the University Christian Unions, and also various women's outreach programmes. I had just begun to feel that, after twenty years 'on the road' it was time to begin slowing down, but how could I say 'No'? While the Lord continued to give me reasonably good health, daily fresh visions of Himself and ever-deepening joy in the study of His Word, I felt constrained to keep on keeping on.

A sudden call to help out at Bethany Fellowship in Minneapolis, at their annual 'Deeper Life Convention', where the booked speaker (a pastor from Bosnia) was hindered by the war in his own country and unable to obtain a visa, helped me to re-focus. God blessed me so much through that week of seeking to share His Word, not so much as a direct challenge to missionary involvement, but rather as a call to true holiness of living in our ordinary everyday lives. I began to see that such a presentation of biblical truth would, in itself, lead to missionary challenge without having to verbalise such. Surely as the desire to live more and more like the Lord Jesus, and to be more and more like Him grows in our hearts, He will move us forward into ministry without anyone having to spell it out! Missionary service is so much on the heart of God the Father who sent His Son into the world to die for us, and God the Son who sent us the Holy Spirit to indwell us and empower us for service, and God the Holy Spirit who sends us into the world around us to show forth the love of God.

The trip to Mexico was unforgettable. There was the sheer vastness of that mighty city and the desperate contrast between the 'well-to-do' side and the 'do-without' side. The welcomes I received at the Union Evangelical Church for the first weekend, and then by the WEC family on the other side of the city, were very touching. And I was given liberty to minister to different groups – one was a group of some seventy five missionaries gathered together from all over the city for encouragement, another was a congregation of over 300 on the Sunday morning. Then there was a whole day's retreat with our WEC family at which we concentrated together on the importance of 'being' Christlike, even before 'doing' godly activities. At every meeting God had to touch my heart and speak to me, before I could pass on His Word to others. It was humbling, sometimes exhausting, but always exhilarating!

From Mexico I flew, by an amazingly circuitous route, back to Knoxville, to Cedar Springs Presbyterian Church, for a missionary weekend. And their loving welcome was like an oasis to my thirsty soul. The unbelievable privilege of speaking to over 1,000 at each of two Sunday morning services really was a refreshment and an encouragement for all that lay ahead in that particular tour in the United States.

My Christmas prayer letter to all my loving supporters sums up that year. 'One particular thought has recurred many times during this year. It is summed up in a quotation from Robert Murray McCheyne, '*My people's greatest need is my personal holiness.*' That is to say, no matter how biblically accurate and doctrinally sound my regular teaching, if my daily life is not lived in accordance with, and in practical outworking of, the theory, the latter will fall on deaf ears. I realise that that is only one side of the truth, but it was a side that the Lord emphasised to me over and over again at that stage in my own journey. And I began speaking more and more on that theme.

My heart was being thrilled, as God continued to direct my ministry to bible teaching, without my being narrowed down to one particular emphasis. I had the joy of a week of teaching in our own church, on the 'Whys' in the life of our Lord Jesus. Why was He born of the Virgin Mary? Why was He, the Holy Son of God, baptised? Why did He do so many miracles, and yet often say 'Tell no-one!'? Why did He have to be crucified on the cruel cross of Calvary? Why did He rise again? Shortly afterwards, when invited to speak at our GCU Annual Leaders' Conference, we thought through the biblical concept of worship. A quotation from a former Archbishop of Canterbury, William Temple, had come into my hands, and certainly enriched my own concept of worship. '*For true worship, we must: (a) quicken the conscience by the holiness of God, (b) feed the mind with the truth of God, (c) purge the imagination by the beauty of God, (d) open the heart to the love of God, and (e) devote the will to the purpose of God.*' On several occasions in the following months I had the opportunity to go through those five points as five steps to be taken into the fullness of worship.

Then there came an invitation to go to another mission's annual field conference and to be with a lovely group of thirty dedicated missionaries, all working in a very hostile and difficult climate. They had come apart for a time of refreshment and renewal, for a period of sharing and praying together. What a privilege to be with them! They were so hungry to see a breakthrough in the barren lands where they served, and so willing to pay any price needful to see this come about. Morning by morning we thought through the training Elijah needed before God could entrust him with the mighty outpouring of fire from on high on Mount Carmel. And each evening we meditated on the last verse of Paul's letter to the Corinthians: '*The **grace** of our Lord Jesus Christ, the **love** of God, and the **fellowship** of the Holy Spirit, be with **us all**. Amen.*' It was so good just to take unhurried time to ponder on the amazing grace of God in sending Jesus into the world to die in our place, to save us from our sins. We thought of the love of God, that despite us being His enemies and choosing to ignore or disobey Him, He so loved us that He gave His only-begotten beloved Son to die for us. And we were blessed as we thought of the fellowship that He offers us with the Godhead, by filling us with the indwelling Holy Spirit, the very Spirit of Christ.

In 1997, my friend and colleague, Pat, and I had the wonderful joy of sharing in another of our WEC Fields' annual conferences, when we spent time every morning and evening meditating on John's first letter. It was probably written to the scattered Jewish Christians through what is now Turkey, believers harassed and with a sense of foreboding and fear of the persecution about to fall on the young churches at the hands of the Roman tyrants. There was so much in every paragraph of that letter to speak to our own hearts. There was teaching to encourage, warn and support us in times of persecution, loneliness or apparent fruitlessness. So many of our Christian brothers and sisters in that land were under stress, being watched daily, often being threatened, never knowing from what side the next attack would come. It was amazing to stand alongside them and enter a little into their heart-agony and yearning.

Pat was invited to share with them on the theme 'Coping with stress'. As she prayed and prepared this message beforehand, the Lord led her to the realisation that it is really *learning to live in the presence of stress*, rather than learning how to cope with it. Her words were so blessed to all of us. She also based her thoughts on the story of Elijah, especially the later episode after the victory on Mount Carmel, when Elijah fled from Jezebel because he was afraid of being killed. He felt weary, discouraged and a failure despite the enormous victory (or more likely, because of it). Pat then led us through three basic steps, or essential principles, in learning to live in the presence of stress. Firstly, there is the detachment of prayer. Secondly, there is the discernment of priorities, and thirdly, the discipline of pain. Each part was illustrated from Scripture and from the writings of others, such as a poem by Amy Carmichael of Dohnavur:

> *'Hast thou no scar? No hidden scar*
> *on foot or side or hand?*
> *I hear thee sung as mighty in the land,*
> *I hear them hail thy bright ascendant star*
> *- Hast thou no scar?'*

Pat illustrated so simply, and yet with such telling reality, that we must accept all that the Lord allows to come into our lives. Another of Amy Carmichael's poems reminds us that 'In acceptance lieth peace.' Is it not indeed a privilege to be invited by our Lord to share in the fellowship of His sufferings? Not only should we accept this, but we should also embrace it.

At the close of that year, as I wrote my Christmas letter, once again I felt a wave of discouragement despite all the blessing of the year, and there had been many. Although I knew I was very tired, I allowed the feelings of discouragement to make me wonder if I was still in line with God's perfect will for my life.

I dreaded that I might just keep going out of habit, even if I was no longer in His will. One morning I asked God for a specific word of fresh direction for the in-coming year. My reading that morning was in 2 Chronicles 15, and verse seven seemed to jump out at me. *'But as for you, be strong and do not give up, for your work will be rewarded.'* How gracious of the dear Lord! I knew I was to press on towards the goal of pleasing Him, day in and day out, preaching the Word in season and out of season. But I also knew that I had to learn not to be so easily swayed by feelings. It is easy to say that to others, but I was so slow to learn the lesson myself – allowing myself to feel self-pity, to feel insecure, to feel that what I was doing was self-pleasing, even self-indulgent, rather than pleasing to God.

I re-read the notes of Pat's words to those missionaries on 'Learning to live in the presence of stress' and felt convicted by how little I had really learned of this lesson myself. To acknowledge that my life was stressful – not because of danger or open opposition, so far as I was personally concerned, but rather because of the sheer pace of living, travelling, meeting with so many people, of other people's expectations, and of seeking to be always ready to fit into any and every situation that arose – was probably half the battle. Having done that, I had to honestly commit the whole to God in believing prayer, seeking His help to set realistic goals for the in-coming year (which had to include learning how to say 'No' graciously!), and accepting His plan even if there was pain involved, realising that it is a privilege to be invited by the Lord to share in His sufferings for this sin-sick world and the desperate need of millions to hear the gospel of His redeeming love.

Chapter Twelve

~~~~~~

Digging Ditches from East to West, from North to South.

The next few years were filled with conferences involving many different nationalities, and with four or five Bible studies at each conference. It really was very exciting. How good God was to give me His word of encouragement to keep on keeping on, and not to grow weary in His service, whether I saw results or not. And throughout the travelling it was amazing how many individuals came up to me to thank me for some word given during the past *twenty* years, 'a word,' they would say, 'that was just for me'. Often they said that they were where they are now because of the challenge of God to their hearts at that time. Though I shouldn't have needed such encouragements, how gracious of God to give them to me to help me keep on keeping on.

It was a very humbling experience to be invited to different WEC sending bases as well as several different Annual Field Conferences to minister a word of encouragement and challenge to our often hard-pressed missionaries, some in situations of considerable danger and/or loneliness. I had been to our WEC families in Hong Kong and in Singapore in 1992 and I went again two years later, together with my friend Pat. We enjoyed such lovely fellowship in the homes of our missionaries and were excited to see the tremendous potential among the young life in both areas. A youth meeting, with over 1,000 teens and early twenties, sat 'eating out of our hands' as we shared the challenge of the unreached millions around the world still waiting to hear the gospel for the very first time. Churches were packed Sunday by Sunday, mostly with young folk, often with very young pastors seeking to lead them on in the Christian faith. They seemed so vibrant; it was as though they were just waiting for the challenge to personal involvement in overseas cross-cultural missions.

Then there was a second visit to Mexico City with its teeming millions. It was a huge joy to speak in a new 'indigenous' church in the centre of the city where there was already some 3,000 members, and where they had started their own Bible school to train national pastors. They were praying that one in every ten students would be called of God into overseas cross-cultural ministry. It was a great opportunity to share with those particular students, basing our thoughts on Luke 5:1-11, (a) the crowd following Jesus representing the needy world 'out there' desperate to hear His voice, (b) the huge catch of fish, representing God's power to bring to birth a church in every people group in the world, and (c) Peter, the reluctant disciple, whom God chose to 'need' for the fulfilment of His purposes. Were we willing to say 'Yes' to the Lord's call to '*launch out into the deep*' (Luke 5:4 KJV) to '*let down the nets*' in what we might think of as the most unlikely place at quite the wrong time of day, and to trust Him to know best? He who made the fish knew exactly where they were, and how they could be caught! What an encouragement to us, the often reluctant 'fishers-of-men'!

After an amazing three-day church retreat focussing on the *grace* of God, who invited us to accept – who entrusted to us – the responsibility of telling others of His love and almighty provision for all our needs, I then had a lovely day with our WEC family. There were around twenty of us, and we thought together of the beauty and loveliness of our Lord and Saviour Jesus as the Treasure, and of ourselves as the jars of clay (2 Cor. 4:7). He moulds us, prepares us and fires us in order to send us wheresoever, and for whatsoever. There were precious times of personal chatting together through some deep problems and seeking His grace to be willing to be 'fired' as He saw fit and needful.

Each year there were so many opportunities to talk of our Lord Jesus, of the grace of God, and of the unbelievable wonder of being called into His service at Bible schools across America and Britain, and at churches and women's groups at home and abroad. I well remember spending time preparing three Bible studies on Moses, based on Hebrews 11:24-27, He *chose* to suffer, '*to be ill-treated along with the people of God rather than to enjoy the pleasures of sin for a short time. He chose to believe. 'He regarded disgrace for the sake of Christ as of greater value than the treasures of Egypt.'* And he *chose* to endure. '*He left Egypt, not fearing the king's anger; he persevered because he saw him who is invisible.'* The time spent in preparation was such a blessing to my own heart! God actually gives us the privilege of making those choices as His Holy Spirit in us draws us to obey Him, and as we are willing to choose to suffer (if needs be) in obeying His will, rather than going with the crowd. If we are willing to choose to believe in Him and His goodness and in His almighty power and ability to keep us whatever befalls, rather than being drawn away to trust in this world's goods and glory, then God will bless us. If we are willing to forego a settled income and the option of promotion, if we are willing to keep on keeping on even in the face of opposition or apparent failure or fruitlessness, then God will bless us, fill us with His peace and joy, and His enabling. What a wonderful God we serve!

There was a small Christian fellowship in Cornwall (the county of my roots, as my American friends would say!) where we had five tremendous sessions together facing the challenge of missions worldwide, under the old titles 'Why?' 'Where?' 'What?' 'Who?' and 'How?'. Then I was invited to East Germany not long after the fall of the Berlin Wall for a 'Deeper Life' conference of workers of Campus Crusade in Europe. Once again, the Lord led us to the ministry of Elijah on Mount Carmel, but I sensed

Him changing the emphasis from the extraordinary event they all saw when the fire fell from heaven on the prepared sacrifice, to the meticulous preparation in the heart and life of Elijah, making him a 'fit instrument' in the hands of the Lord. It was also very humbling to meet up with nationals of Eastern Europe, so long separated from us by a wall of man's making, and to sense their deep love of the Lord. No amount of persecution or threatening had been able to extinguish the spark of holy fire. I was given a beautiful gift at the close of the conference, a gift that I have treasured ever since and that is brought out every Christmas. It is a hand-carved manger scene under an arch with five candleholders. Beautiful in its simplicity, it is also amazing in the delicacy of its workmanship.

That was followed by a trip back to the USA for ten days packed with meetings, including three days at the Nanibijou Conference Centre, where I have made dear friends over the years. There were many there who had been deeply hurt and whose minds were bruised by a sad occurrence in the church fellowship to which they belonged, and I was specifically asked to minister to the question 'Why does a God of love allow suffering?' This was the question that I had been challenged to answer years earlier when in Australia. God led me then to realise that it is *because* He **is** a God of love that *He* suffered for us, and that now He invites *us* to share in His sufferings. As then, so it is now. We did not actually come up with an answer to the initial question, but rather we reached some understanding of the unquestioning acceptance of a life of sharing in the fellowship of His sufferings. If we love deeply we can expect to suffer deeply as well.

And so to Africa! Pat and I were invited to Malawi, where my youngest sister and her husband taught in the secondary school at Livingstonia. Robin and Frances were deeply involved in the restoration of the church building that had been started by Dr Laws, a Presbyterian missionary, early in the 1900s, but had sadly never been completed. We had played a small part in encouraging folk to give financially to this project. So when it was nearing completion, we were invited to go out for the dedication service. This certainly was a very different kind of ministry. What a beautiful country Malawi is, right there in the heart of the vast continent of Africa! We were given a royal welcome and we enjoyed every moment of our time there. The church was packed for the dedication with two separate choirs of younger and older singers. All the workmen who had been involved in the restoration and building programme were there, as were visiting Presbyterian missionaries and leaders from other parts of Malawi. I was invited to say a few words of spiritual encouragement. I spoke on the fact that God is more deeply desirous of the completion of building His temple in the hearts and lives of His people, even than in the bricks and mortar building in which we were sitting (1 Cor. 3:16). There was a hush over that huge congregation and we sensed a willingness in some to be challenged to put God first in their lives.

For all my travels over the years I had never been to mainland China. However, I *was* invited to minister at the Easter Convention of Chinese students studying at various universities in the east of the UK. As so often, I found it very humbling to see the intense interest of over 100 young students as we worked our way through 1 Corinthians 15:1-11. On Good Friday, '*Christ died for our sins*' (15:3) reminded us of all His death means for us and to us. He died as our substitute, 'in my place, condemned, He stood'. We sought to take a new grasp of the wonder and magnitude of the gospel, reminding ourselves that there is '*no other name under heaven given to men by which we must be saved*' (Acts 4:12). On the Saturday, when our subject was that '*He was buried*', we thought of the more than two billion people in our world today who are still waiting to hear the gospel, considering not only their geographic distribution but their needs, and the countless opportunities we have to meet those needs. On Easter Sunday, '*He was raised on the third day*' was the glorious truth we studied. We revelled in the marvel of the resurrection, worshipped the Lamb in many glorious Easter hymns, and sought to realise afresh something of what His resurrection means to us. It is our ultimate assurance that Christ dying for us on the cross was acceptable to the Father as our propitiation. On the Monday, we thought about the various appearances of the Lord after His resurrection, first to Peter and the Twelve, then to the 500 brethren gathered together and to James, and lastly, to Paul in that wonderful meeting on the road to Damascus. From that meeting Paul, a completely changed man, went out to *carry God's name before the Gentiles and their kings*' (Acts 9:15). Are we prepared, we asked ourselves, to be completely changed, re-created by God in the likeness of our Lord and Saviour, and sent out by Him to witness to all peoples? The responsiveness of those young people was almost overwhelming. They were indeed 'prepared vessels', ready for the challenge.

Immediately following that weekend, I went to the headquarters of the Overseas Missionary Fellowship (OMF), to meet up with a selected group from GCU: Ruth Hodgson, a Leader from Glasgow, and four young university students: Elaine from Northern Ireland; Rachel, the daughter of missionary parents working in Thailand; Hannah from a university in the Midlands of England, and Maddy from Wales. We were there to prepare for 'the experience of a lifetime!' as one expressed it, after our summer excursion. We were going together as a team to Thailand and Vietnam to experience what it means to 'be a missionary', in as far as that is possible in six short weeks! These two countries were chosen for their contrasts. One is an 'open' country, but with little response, the other is a supposed 'closed' country where, in fact, there is an eagerness to hear the gospel.

We had two days of orientation and teaching to seek to prepare us for living in another culture, amidst a people of another language. It was a good two days. We got to know each other a bit, and began to gel together. We thought of various aspects of how we should behave in the two countries we were to visit, seeing ourselves as servants of the people, and being willing to learn from them as well as longing to pass on to them the truths of the gospel. I shared the 'five vowels of Christian discipline – specifically in the life of a young missionary.' A, accepting the authority of those over us in the Lord, in the main without questioning. E, enjoying the experience as a gift from God, and seeking always to help each other and our host missionaries to enjoy having us, by thoughtfulness and helpfulness. I, the essential need to cross out our individuality, our 'I', as in Galatians 2:20, so that it may truly be said of each one of us: '*I have been crucified with Christ and I no longer live, but Christ lives in me.*' O, obeying all orders promptly, knowing that those who have been there for years know better than we do how we should behave in certain situations – such as the advice we had been given about the clothes we should or should not wear. And U, be understanding, slow to criticise but quick to listen, and to seek to enter into the lives of those we were there to serve – missionaries, as well as nationals. When we return home, we noted, we were to be quick to express appreciation, and very slow to express criticisms, knowing that God would give us understanding hearts as we asked Him.

On the 15th July 2000, we were ready to leave the UK and to launch out into the deep, not without trepidation, yet full of excited expectations. From our meeting together at Heathrow airport, and the celebration of Maddy's birthday (she was the youngest member of our team) to the day, six weeks later, that we said our goodbyes to each other, again at Heathrow airport, it was indeed a fantastic experience. We were all so conscious of the prayerful upholding every day by a veritable army of supporters from each of our six families, our home churches and the GCU family throughout the UK. And we were almost overwhelmed by the generous kindness of our hosts. The stretched, and often overworked, team of OMF missionaries in both Thailand and Vietnam were marvellous. We were met at Bangkok airport and driven north by Eunice Burden to Lop Buri, the OMF language school and centre for initial orientation of new missionaries. They allowed us to take part in some basic lessons in speaking Thai.

The girls really worked at this and did well. But my ears and tongue were simply not as quick as theirs!

Snippets from my diary of the visit might have read, 'Down town shopping... finding our way around by maps rather than by enquiring... eating in local cafes... coming to terms with sticky heat... the privilege of sharing with all the local OMF personnel... taken further up-country to the OMF medical centre at Manorom... touring the hospital and local village... further privilege of sharing with the team of doctors and nurses, and then of speaking at the local church.' Everywhere we walked we saw idols of the Buddha, and we could feel the heaviness of spiritual darkness. We moved to Uthai, to stay with Jan Trelogan. Once again a generous welcome awaited us. Jan moved out of her bedroom, so that Ruth and I could enjoy that comfort, including the fan to cool us down in the hot sticky nights (just as Eunice had done for me in Lop Buri). Then started the 'service' that we had come for – teaching English in an enormous state secondary school, with 1,800 pupils in ten streams in each of six years! How we thanked God that Ruth was a seasoned teacher and knew how to encourage the four girls to prepare for and deliver their teaching! None of the rest of us had much idea. By the end of ten intensive days the girls were just beginning to enjoy the experience.

The four girls lived in Thai homes, ate Thai food and travelled on the back of motorbikes in true Thai fashion! They taught several classes a day to all the different age groups, made many friends and really began to integrate into the local culture. At the end of our time at that school we were treated like royalty. Presentations were made to each of us by the Principal, before the whole assembled school. A party in the school and another (including a karaoke of 1960s Beatles' songs!) with staff members at a local hotel were some of the highlights before we moved on to our next assignment, with our hearts overflowing with praise to God for all His abundant goodness to us.

During the time that Ruth and the girls were teaching at Uthai, I had the opportunity to travel over two hours further north to Tak, to spend three days with our WEC family at yet another minifield conference. There were many opportunities for ministry and encouragement to the whole group, in smaller groups and to individuals, as well as in the small but vibrant local church. Once again I was filled with an awed sense of humble worship at God's condescension in allowing me any part in such a ministry. As we saw and sensed the enormous difficulties of presenting the gospel in a country soaked in Buddhism, with the attendant threat of a sense of failure, of fruitlessness, of 'is it really worthwhile?' the Lord led us all to concentrate on the fact that it is HIS work, not ours. He calls us to a life of holiness and trust, a life lived in the belief that He is fulfilling His perfect plan, even if we cannot see how. As I mentioned in the last chapter, the words of McCheyne had become very meaningful to me in the previous year or two, 'My people's greatest need is my personal holiness.' We are called to reflect the Lord's beauty through our lives as much as through our words, and God will use this in His own perfect time. 'We have this treasure (the lovely Lord Jesus) in jars of clay', but those jars need to be absolutely clean, fired and filled, so that the overflow may be seen by others.

On travelling back to Bangkok, once again we were welcomed by the OMF personnel at their guesthouse. We had two days to relax and refresh, to see the sights of Bangkok and to go out to lunch with Ruth's brother in a smart downtown hotel, where eating rice was thankfully not mandatory! There was also shopping and the celebration of Rachel's birthday! Then we flew on to Vietnam to be met at Ho Chi Minh City airport by two OMF missionaries. As everywhere, they put themselves out to welcome us and help us settle into yet another new situation. We were to stay at Lan Anh Hotel right in the tourist area of the city. As our four lovely rooms had air conditioning and en suite bathrooms, we had ample opportunity to scrub our filthy feet after frequently being barefoot (in accordance with local culture) in Thailand!

On the Sunday, we walked together along the bustling street to church, passing hundreds of small shops crowded with vendors and their tricycles, and noisy with the roar of motorbikes. It was a large airy building seating some 400 people. The congregation was celebrating the 75th anniversary of missionaries from the Christian and Missionary Alliance founding the work in Vietnam in 1925. There were to be three services that morning to accommodate the over 1,000 members. Several choirs, of every age group, led the worship and the singing was beautiful. We heard an excellent sermon by the senior pastor, on Numbers 21:4-9, the remedy for being bitten by a fiery serpent was to look up to the image of a serpent, made by Moses, and raised on a pole in the centre of the Israelites' camp, in accordance with the Word of God. The teaching was so clear. It was wonderful to have fellowship with local believers in such an open and unharassed way, though no foreigner may today take any part in the leadership of the church in Vietnam. We heard that there are some twenty other similar churches throughout Ho Chi Minh City. This was all such a contrast to what we had seen in the Buddhist stronghold of Thailand, and so different from our expectations.

Throughout our three weeks in Thailand, Ruth led our group each day in prayer for what lay ahead of us, and in Bible study in Mark's Gospel, with notebooks that she had prepared for us beforehand. In Vietnam it was my privilege to lead that daily prayer time, and we started a Bible study on how God changed Simon into Peter. I think each of us had times of feeling very much like Simons, and of asking God to complete His work in us, His work of making us into Peters.

Each day we enjoyed eating out at a local restaurant/café. A good meal of rice and pork, with a large milk shake made from local fruits, cost the princely sum of £1! We went shopping in the market and managed to pick up lots of small souvenirs to take home. The girls made use of a local 'internet café' to send and receive e-mails. We had a wonderful outing to the Mekong River and a boat trip across it to a coconut plantation where we watched the process of extracting all the goodness from coconuts and the making of coconut sweetmeats. Then we saw the shells being carved into ornaments for exporting.

One of the OMF missionaries tried hard to find a 'way in' to a local school where we could teach English, but this was not as easily arranged as in Thailand. We had to be patient. But then came the news that we could go to a small private school for 15 to 30-year-olds wishing to learn English. It was a conversational arrangement rather than a formal classroom situation. The 'students' were at all stages, from some who knew practically no English at all, to a couple going on to university, who already had a fairly good grasp of basic English. All six of us were to be involved, with Ruth very definitely our coordinator-cum-leader! I wrote in my diary that evening, 'I dread to think how we would cope without Ruth. She just *is* a teacher, and so patient with us, willing to guide, help and encourage us!'

During our first evening at the school, we broke up into small groups and got to know each other. We shared, as far as they were able to understand, about our homes and ourselves. Then we played games using the little English they knew. From then on it was to be more intensive! We prepared dialogues, taught a little bit of grammar, engaged in conversational pieces, and made up a story about shopping involving the prices of fruit and vegetables. Maddy and I worked together with five students of 'middle ability'. All groups were taught in the same small room, and Maddy and I did not find this easy. Everyone talked loudly and laughed a lot. It was not exactly the best atmosphere for serious teaching. Each evening we spent an hour or more thinking out what we would teach the next day, preparing material, photocopying crosswords, maps, word-searches, block-busters, noughts and crosses, choruses – anything to increase vocabulary and encourage our students to try out their English.

At the end of our ten days with them, we all gave each other a fantastic farewell party! The school Director, with his own class of students, plus three other members of staff at the school, joined us. We had a hilarious time. Everyone joined in and seemed to enjoy themselves tremendously. Speeches were made, presents given, certificates presented, and then came the 'eats' in a mixture of Vietnamese and European. Having eaten, photos were taken, addresses swapped and quite tearful goodbyes said. There was genuine emotion on all sides, including a letter from one of the staff (unable to come to the party) saying that our presence had made 'this school a different place'. She thought 'it must be your God.'

Although our time at the school was ended, we still had another exciting adventure ahead of us. A Christian travel agent organised a trip up-country into the mountains, to DaLat, with a group of students (most of whom were not Christians) who all wanted to improve their English. Two leaders (at least one of whom was truly a Christian) and thirteen young people aged from 14 to 24 years, all piled into a 24-seater coach with us and all our luggage. Introductory remarks and welcomes were followed by a few songs to a guitar accompaniment, and then we all fell asleep as we drove north through a tropical downpour. Eventually we arrived at a hotel in DaLat, settled into our nice and very adequate rooms, before spending the evening together. By the time we had been for a walk, stopped at a coffee shop and played some party games, we were beginning to know each other's names. Ruth kept everything going and under control. Two older people in the group, a man aged 16 and a lady of 24, were definitely seeking to know more about spiritual matters and they asked about our reason for being there. On the second afternoon, despite heavy rain, we went on an excursion that involved walking up hundreds of steps, through an alleyway of stalls all selling the same 'tourist-icky' articles, across the plateau, and down the far side of the 'mountain' to a lake. Then, despite the continuing rain, we set off, in two motorboats to tour the lake. At the far side, the 'driver' of our boat allowed us to disembark and clamber up a slippery, muddy hillside, where we discovered enormous models of animals: giraffes, camels, bullocks, rhinoceros, all two by two. Suddenly, as we reached the top of the hillside, we saw straight in front of us two huge statues of Adam and Eve! It was so totally unexpected that we laughed. One of the Vietnamese group who was with us, 24-year-old Phon, asked if we knew who these two people were? That started a truly amazing conversation that continued, on and off, throughout the next two days, and all the way back down to Ho Chi Minh City. Phon was hungry to know all that we could tell her, not only of Adam and Eve, but also of our Creator God, and all that is written in His Book. She never ceased to ply us all with questions. Ruth and Hannah spent hours with her, and slowly her heart opened up – like Lydia's in Acts 16 – to receive the Lord as her Saviour.

On our arrival back at the city, as we said goodbye to each other at the Travel Agent's shop, Phon looked straight at us. With a lovely smile, she said, 'We will meet again – if not here, then in glory!' We realised, in almost stunned amazement, just how much she had already received from God in understanding the gospel. That was truly the 'icing on the cake' for all of us. Phon's conversion was the best possible gift God could have given us as our time in Vietnam drew to a close.

We all felt so full of gratitude to God for those amazing six weeks. In our last Bible study together, we looked at John 4, the woman who met Jesus at the well, and we wondered if Phon was our 'woman at the well' – thirsty, ready and responsive. Had we been in Vietnam because the Holy Spirit knew that we *must* go through that way in order to meet that young woman?

As I look back over all that I have recorded in this chapter, and ask myself, 'Lord, what were you teaching *me*? Have I learned the lesson?' Surely above all else, the Lord was saying, 'I am able!' He *is* in control. I don't need to panic. I don't need to tell Him what I think I can or cannot do. I can trust Him in *every* situation, even if I may be faced with totally unknown and unexpected moments. It is not for me to dictate to the Lord how I want to serve Him, nor where. He is a much better judge of that than I am. I am so full of thankfulness to the Lord for

His overwhelming goodness, His enabling, His strength and His vision, and I just want to go on going on, to know Him better, to love Him more dearly and to keep following Him to the end of the journey.

Chapter Thirteen

Still Digging Ditches – not yet a Suez Canal!

Immediately following my exciting trip to South East Asia, Pat and I went away for a short holiday. We needed to be refreshed and renewed, physically and spiritually, before a new year of activities began. Unfortunately, I went down with a chest infection and was quite sick. It cannot have been much of a holiday for Pat as I struggled to regain strength. But it taught me, once again, how frail we are apart from the Lord's enabling, and how utterly dependent we are on Him every day for His sustaining grace.

Back home, we were immediately into vigorous preparation for a tour of meetings of Bible schools in central and western Canada. I never cease to marvel at the Lord's grace in allowing us to minister among these keen young Christians. Some of the schools were fairly large with over 500 students and others were smaller with 150 or so. At some I was invited to minister four or five times over several days, at others once or twice in one day. Travelling between the schools sometimes involved one or two air flights or long car journeys through the prairies. But everywhere there were such warm welcomes and such intense and eager interest. At the first college we worked our way, as on some previous occasions, through the prophecy of Jonah, looking at (a) how to find God's will for our lives, (b) the need of prayer and obedience to God if we are to know and act on His will for our lives, (c) the urgent need of the world of today to hear the gospel message, and (d) our motivation in our service – to see God glorified, and not simply to please ourselves, and certainly not to receive the praise of men.

At other colleges we spent more time concentrating on our need to be clean mirrors, reflecting the loveliness of Jesus all day every day, no matter what the outward circumstances. I shared with them that instead of asking ourselves 'Is it worth it?' when the way gets tough, and our backs are to the wall, we should ask 'Is He worthy?' There will certainly, eventually, come a day when we will be tempted to say 'No' to the first question, but the second will always bring us round to saying 'Yes. One hundred times yes!' At the last college we visited there was freezing snow on the ground, but the warmth in the students' hearts was a tremendous contrast. Five meetings were held there, from a classroom situation with some thirty to a chapel period with all 300 students. The smaller group focussed on relationships on the mission field, and the larger on the fact that the world's deepest need is to see Christ in Christians who live holy lives that reflect His loveliness and goodness.

Back home again, Pat and I received an unexpected invitation to go to visit and encourage two different groups of workers in two neighbouring countries in the '10/40 window' area of the world – probably in February of 2002. [For reasons of security these countries will not be named in this narrative.] We began praying about this request, seeking clear guidance from the Lord. Should we go or not? We did not wish our decision to be made according to the safety and/or risk that such a journey would entail, nor according to our desires or otherwise, but simply, was this God's voice to us? Meanwhile there were plenty of engagements closer to home. The list included teaching a small group of older teens every Sunday in our GCU Group, a group of ladies every Wednesday morning in our church, a sizeable collection of students at a university Christian Union houseparty in Wales and an exciting group of nearly 100 young people at an outreach weekend organised by OMF in Ireland. There were opportunities in our Belfast and Coleraine University Christian Unions, various Anglican Mothers' Union meetings and Presbyterian Women's Association gatherings.

At the same time, Pat and I together were becoming deeply involved in another ministry for our local church. Our minister, after over twenty years of devoted service, often despite ill health, had to retire. There was a vacancy. In the Church of Ireland the local congregation chooses four members as 'nominators' to search for a new minister who is able and willing to come and fill their needs of pastoral care and faithful biblical teaching. Pat and I were two of those four in our church. For six months this involved us in writing letters, visiting other churches to hear ministers preaching, and meeting with our Bishop and the four nominators he had appointed to discuss and pray over our needs.

In the midst of all this activity, in April 2001, we went together on a visit to South Africa. That in itself was quite a story! A phone call came to us a year previously, and a man's voice said, 'This is John Carter!' Who was John Carter? Why was I expected to know him? And where was he phoning from? He told me that he was ringing from South Africa, and that this call was the result of years he had spent trying to find me. Why? I wondered. He told me that, in 1964, he was one of the mercenary soldiers who rescued me from the 'Simba Uprising,' (the civil war) that erupted so mercilessly in Congo that August. Something in me stood still. Did I want to be reminded of all that had taken place that dreadful year? John went on talking, saying that through that day's rescue of the ten Protestant missionaries (our WEC family, working in that part of the world at the time) and through our testimonies, our whole attitude, and the apparent lack of any hatred or anger, he had become a Christian! I could hardly believe my ears! John wanted to make contact. He wanted to meet me. But I couldn't respond quite so quickly. I needed time to take it in and to know if I truly wanted to open up the past.

Some months later, and following further telephone conversations with John and with Stuart Rising, another of the same mercenary group, we got a phone call to tell us that John, and his wife Rona, were in Northern Ireland, at a Bed and Breakfast establishment near the port through which they had arrived the previous day! We drove across and spent a day with the two of them, Rona with Pat in her car, and John with me in his hired car. We talked! We filled in a lot of history of all that had taken place in our lives in the intervening thirty years since our first meeting. When we said goodbye to them, they pressed us to accept their invitation to visit them in South Africa.

During the months that followed, John had a recurrence of a previous cancerous condition, and sadly, in January 2001, he died before we managed to visit them. But his dying wish was that we would, nevertheless, go out to visit his home. As Rona and their daughter echoed that wish we made the necessary preparations and in April we went. Met by Rona, we were driven northwest from Durban, up to her home in Hilton, near Pietermaritzburg. Interestingly enough, my own brother and his wife had lived for two years in that small town of Hilton, teaching in the boy's College! We went out to see the college one day, and took photos for me to bring home to Bob and Ione.

Rona organised a tremendous holiday for us. We went for several days on an escorted tour of the battlefields, and we spent three wonderful days in a hotel by the beach south of Durban, spending as much time in the water as out! Then we travelled to Cape Town and stayed with Rona's daughter. From there we took three bus tours in different directions to see something of the beauty and hugeness of the country. Everyone was so kind to us, and made it what one might call 'the holiday of a lifetime'!

Needless to say, on our return to Northern Ireland we had to take up our duties as nominators, looking for a new rector for our parish, meeting regularly for prayer, and reporting on all we heard, and on letters we received. All this activity came to a happy conclusion with the appointment of our present rector.

We learned a considerable amount through all that was involved in the exercise, not least our utter dependence on God for His guidance and assurance each step of the way.

Then suddenly – and I suppose, for everyone, wholly unexpectedly – there was the enormous catastrophe of the 11th September 2001. All ex-patriot workers serving in NGOs in the countries to which we had been invited had to leave and come home. Initially there was no immediate expectation of a return to the countries of their adoption. So all plans were put on hold. That October, I went to Cleveland, Ohio, to minister to a group of 300 women at their annual church retreat. Once more I had such a sense of privilege. They were hungry for all I felt led to share with them. There was a great responsiveness, not just at the five programmed meetings, but also in all the private conversations and at meal tables throughout the weekend. On arriving back in the UK, there was a letter from those workers who had had to be evacuated following the 9/11 events, asking if I would consider going to London to meet with them as they were discussing and praying about their future. As I sat in on all their sessions, I was humbled – awed – to realise their total dedication to the tasks to which God had called them. All were ready to go back to the country of their adoption the moment the way opened up, and the powers-that-be in the Foreign Office agreed to it. None idly dismissed the all-too-obvious dangers, but equally, they did not major on them, and that included the mothers of young children as well as their husbands.

In the daily devotional times, we based our studies on Philippians 3:10: *'I want to know Christ and the power of his resurrection and the fellowship of sharing in his sufferings …'* We linked our studies to each of these three phrases. Firstly, there is our personal relationship with our Lord Jesus Christ, in submission. Secondly, we have our relationship to one another, in service – as He served us, so must we serve others (John 13:14). And thirdly, entering into the suffering of God for those in our world today who are without Him – dying to ourselves that Christ may wholly dwell in us, and so feel through us, act through us, care through us.

2002 brought a renewed invitation to visit our friends who had been enabled to return to their country of service, so that we could see the needs there for ourselves. We were torn. Part of me was deeply attracted and part was afraid. How could I be sure what God was saying? Could I know without doubt that He was telling us to go, and that it was not just my own inclination? Could I trust Him to undertake completely for both of us (I never considered going without Pat's companionship and encouragement!) despite the natural fears in the climate of the day? We both agreed to lay the matter before the Lord and seek a clear word of direction.

Meanwhile, I had a ten-day engagement at a Bible seminary in Mississippi to give five Bible studies at their annual public conference. I was strangely fearful. I just felt I was not the person to be filling such an important role, and that the faculty and students would all be much better trained in biblical exposition than I was. I knew that my reasoning and fears were based on the wrong assumption that God was dependent on my abilities and educational training in order to be able to use me in His service. Although I knew that was not true, once again it was quite a fight to accept God's peace, and to know that what He had put in my heart to share with those seminarians was His choice and not mine, and that He would undertake if I took my hands off and did not look for personal satisfaction in this particular ministry.

I went, and was so warmly welcomed by the family with whom I was to stay. It really was a rebuke for having been afraid. It was the same at the college. The reception of what God wanted to share with them, through me, was overwhelming. Again, I had to accept God's rebuke. 'Could you not trust Me?' Once again we thought through the story of Elijah, of how God sent him to rebuke King Ahab, then hid him and cared for him through months of drought at Brook Kerith before sending him on to the widow at Zarephath. We saw how God directed him to challenge King Ahab and all the prophets of Baal on Mount Carmel before instructing Elijah to rebuild the broken down altar, slay the bullock, set the wood and the bullock on the altar as a sacrifice, pray ... but not to put fire under the sacrifice. Then, as Elijah prayed fearlessly in front of the huge gathered crowd on the mountainside, '... *the fire of the Lord fell and burned up the sacrifice, the wood, the stones and the soil, and also licked up the water in the trench'* (1 Kings 18:38). God spoke to all our hearts about the various conditions that are necessary, today as then, for Him to send down the fire from heaven in mighty revival blessing.

During the ten days I spent in Mississippi I had the joy of ministering in various churches, including to a group of young people and in a local secondary school. But above all, I had the most wonderful fellowship in the home of those who invited me there, with their four delightful young people and two huge friendly dogs! It was a time of deep and real refreshment. How good it was of God to give me that, as well as the privilege of being His mouthpiece at the college.

I arrived home again to another communication from our friends in that faraway nameless country. Would we come to visit them in February 2003? Pat and I talked it over; we sought the Lord's face and, when we read Daily Light for that morning (November 11th), '*He led them on safely*' (Ps. 78:53), we nearly laughed out loud! The next verses confirmed the word of the first: '*I lead in the way of righteousness, in the midst of the paths of judgement*' (Prov. 8:20 AV) followed by: '*Behold, I send an Angel before thee, to keep thee in the way, and to bring thee into the place which I have prepared*' (Ex. 23:20 AV). What more could we possibly need? We bowed our heads, and said, 'Yes, Lord.' We sent a communication to tell our friends of God's word to us and then started preparations in earnest. They let us know what they wanted so far as ministry was concerned: four Bible studies during their annual get-together, possibly two opportunities to share with bigger groups of foreign workers at their Sunday meetings, and a Bible study for a small group of workers who were seeking to go up-country to serve in an almost unreached tribal area. Letters were written to embassy officials seeking visas in our passports. Injections were organised to protect against the most commonly occurring infections, and clothes bought for the cold of winter and to be acceptable to the culture.

The day came when all was ready. Many friends supported us in their prayers, and none actually told us that they thought we were foolhardy 'at our age'. But sometimes the looks we intercepted told us more than their unspoken words! The route of travel had been chosen, and we set off, from Belfast through Heathrow to Germany. After a short delay, we flew on, on two more planes, to our final destination.

There our friends were to meet us! Although our luggage was grossly over the allowed free baggage weight, we were not charged a penny! The luggage included many gifts for the children from their family in Belfast, plus needed electrical tools for Martin. We had to explain at each airport check that the 'things' in our baggage that looked like firearms were actually only tools for helping our friends in their service ministries and, amazingly, we were not made to unpack a thing! Everything went through without a hitch. 'You of little faith, why did you doubt?' Was that what Jesus wanted to say to me? Just as He had told His disciples, that 'they' (Jesus and the disciples) would go to the other side of the lake, had He not clearly told us that 'we' (Jesus and ourselves) were to go over to visit our friends, and that He was sending His angel before us? Why then did I doubt?

What excitement, amidst the encircling snow-covered mountains, as we disembarked at the airport, eventually collected all our luggage, and then drove through the city to our friends' home. The welcome is hard to describe. Saying that it was tremendous does not do it justice! We realised, with a deep sense of unworthiness, that our coming truly was an encouragement to those who might well have felt discouraged at the slowness of change in that vast land of huge needs. Dear Joyce, mother of three lively young boys, made us feel immediately at home. And meals appeared like clockwork despite all the shortcomings of the cooking facilities. Even in the middle of a sharp bout of real winter weather, the home was kept warm despite problems with the heating arrangements. No one complained when the room suddenly filled with billowing black, acrid smoke, and everyone helped to patch up the leaking chimney and then to clean up the sooty mess. The giving and opening of presents appeared 'like a second Christmas' one of the boys exclaimed!

A group gathered over the next day or two, made up of a doctor from the far west of the land, a trained teacher from the far east, and those of the city itself, as well as two senior workers from further afield and ourselves from the UK. All were housed, all were fed and all were kept warm. The informal get-together was soon underway, with hymn-singing to a guitar accompaniment, testimonies from one and another, sharing of problems and heartaches and a godly seeking of solutions. A daily study in the Word was based on the four biblical principles: sacrifice, faith, holiness and fellowship, about which I had by then completed writing four books, and how we must all seek to see these principles worked out in our daily living experience.

Then there was a lovely time together with the small group of four workers who had their hearts drawn to serve in a remote northern region. Our friend Martin was their team leader. The team included three single women, one a doctor from the UK, another a nurse from the USA, and also a male Norwegian logistician. They had asked me to prepare some thoughts on verse nine in the Beatitudes in Matthew 5: '*Blessed are the peacemakers*' as they saw this to be one of the most important parts of their ministry in the future. We thought together of our need to accept the whole standard of all the beatitudes, and not just one isolated verse. We must know ourselves to be spiritually *poor*, unable to achieve anything in our own strength, utterly dependent on God's enabling grace. We must never cease to *mourn* over our frequent failures – our waywardness, our criticisms of others and our pride, our lack of faith and our slowness to grow up into maturity in Christ – so that we can receive and rejoice in His comfort. This must always be accompanied by a *meekness* of spirit, a humility, a knowing that we can never deserve His grace and forgiveness. And that should lead us into a deep *hunger and thirst* after righteousness, an ever-increasing desire to be truly Christlike, to be holy as he is. Such holiness will always result in a *merciful* spirit towards others, a purity of heart towards God and a purposefulness to be always pleasing to Him rather than to one another or to ourselves. Then, from that position, stems the possibility of truly being *peacemakers* – but with the realisation that such a ministry brings the certainty of *persecution*. The devil will not let us alone. He will throw himself into the battle to stop our ministry or to render it ineffective. Has not God specifically told us that any who strive to live godly lives will suffer persecution (2 Tim. 3:12)?

On more than one occasion during the fellowship of those two weeks, I used the experiences of the civil war in Congo in the 1960s to illustrate these truths. One such illustration involved the night in October 1964, when I was beaten up, when the Lord challenged me with the question, 'Can you thank Me for trusting you with this experience, even if I never tell you why?' I tried to explain a little of what this question had come to mean to me. It was as though God had said to me, 'Don't try to reason it out. Trust Me! I have a plan and purpose. I do know what I am doing and what I am asking of you in the fulfilment of My purpose. Can you not thank Me for inviting you to be part of My plan, even if you never understand the Why?' I shared my testimony of how, in the midst of that terrible night, with very little understanding of what God was actually saying to me, I managed to say, 'OK, God, if this is in Your plan, thank You for letting me be a part of it,' and how, immediately, He flooded my heart with His peace despite the continuing pain and brutality.

Several months after we returned home from those two weeks we heard an amazing story. Immediately after we left, the small team went the three-day journey north and had a very successful visit of the region, setting up a small mobile medical clinic to help the people there. Around three months later, some of the team went back with their local helpers for three weeks of ministry. As they were leaving on mule-back, they were attacked by two young tribesmen who drove away their national helpers at gunpoint. They then fired shots round the girls, beat them with sticks and forced them to climb up the steep rough mountainside, goading them on with their guns if they stumbled or hesitated. What lay ahead? Cruelty? Torture? Death?

Suddenly, local people appeared on the scene and rescued the captives. Their national helpers had gone to find others to join them and to follow the marauders, in order to bring the girls back to safety. They achieved this, and the girls were practically unhurt. But what of their thoughts? What of the mental strain of such an ordeal? How did they stand up to that? When questioned, they shared how at the beginning of the incident they had a brief opportunity to pray together, and they committed themselves to God before being forced to start their gruelling ascent. They could see by their captors' eyes that at least one of the men was capable of killing them. Indeed, they found out later that he had previously killed eight people, including some of his own relatives.

Their minds turned to one thought – as they were later to tell each other. Knowing, and almost expecting, that they might die, they felt the Lord ask, 'Can you thank Me for trusting you with this experience even if I never tell you why?' They went on to tell how they experienced no fear throughout the hours of their capture – only the peace of Christ – the Christ who had promised to be with them always, in life and in death. Isn't God wonderful? I never cease to wonder at His perfect timing, and at how He can prompt us to say what He wants said, and at just the right time. I was awed and humbled to have been a small part of that remarkable story, and I thank God for giving me the privilege of sharing with others His teaching and prompting under so many different circumstances.

Later the same year, Pat and I had a traumatic experience, and I was tested regarding the reality of my own testimony. Did I speak only from my head, or was it honestly from deep down inside my innermost being? At 2.20 a.m. one morning, I went from my bedroom, across the small corridor in our home, to the bathroom. I had not put on my glasses, but I did notice a light on in the hall. Had I forgotten to turn off one of the lights at bedtime? When I went to investigate, the light went out. I stepped into the sitting room doorway to glance out the windows. Had someone's security light gone on and off? I looked, but did not notice any movement outside. Then, when I turned back, thinking to go to the kitchen and get a drink of water, I became conscious of an 'object' in the hall, and wondered what Pat had left there. Suddenly, the 'object' exploded, leapt up, hands waving, and crashed towards me. Utterly devastated, I fell back against the wall in the corridor and the intruder rushed past me and out through the French windows in the study into the dark night. He must have left them open for his get away.

Finding my voice out of my shock and horror, I yelled for Pat to come. 'There's a man in the house!' We rang for police and the rest of the night passed in a blur. In my heart a voice seemed to say, 'Can you thank God now?' and I shrank away from the voice. For several days I would not even listen to the challenge in that question. Yet, even in my refusal to listen, I felt condemned. Was I for real, or was my testimony always past tense? For several nights I relived the horror of that experience. I could not sleep peacefully. Would the intruder come back? I wondered. We heard from the police that on several occasions in our area, where people had been 'disturbed' at night, the intruder returned some weeks later. Would that happen to us? Would it be worse next time?

When the police first arrived, I had almost triumphantly said, 'No-one was hurt!' I was sure that God had protected us, but would He protect us next time round? My mind went over and over the events. I tormented myself, and was unable to let go and relax into His grace and goodness. I just could not bring myself to thank Him for trusting me with this. Security people came and readjusted the alarm system so that it could be used when we were in the house as well as when we went out. A new lock was put on the French window in the study, and also on the back door into the garage. Banks replaced all our stolen credit cards and refunded the money stolen from them. Everyone was so kind, doing all they could to restore my equilibrium. Our neighbours gave us their telephone numbers and told us not to hesitate to call them any hour, day or night, if we needed help.

Three days after the event, my reading in Daily Light started with: '*We know that all things work together for good to them that love God*' (Rom. 8:28). I held on to that. A few days later it was: '*Beloved, think it not strange concerning the fiery trial which is to try you ...*' (1 Pet. 4:12). I prayed earnestly that I would be willing to learn whatever God wanted to teach me through this incident. Then in reading, on October 1st, from *My Utmost for His Highest* by Oswald Chambers, the text for that day was, '*Jesus took Peter and James and John with him, and led them up a high mountain, where they were all alone.*' I was challenged to rethink that prayer, to be willing to learn whatever the Lord wanted to teach me through the recent horrific incident. Chambers wrote, 'We are apt to think that everything that happens is to be turned into useful teaching – no! – it is to be turned into something better than teaching; it is to be turned into character. The (momentous moments in our lives) are not meant to *teach* us anything, they are meant to *make* us something.'

It was hard indeed to think of that terrifying moment at 2.20 a.m. on the 18th September as a 'mountain top' experience. And yet, in a sense, it was. It was driving me to re-evaluate my living, ongoing relationship with God. How completely was I given over to Him, accepting a daily dying of my self-life that He might more and more fully indwell me, possess me, control my thinking, my emotions, my reactions in every part? Suddenly it all slipped into place, and I knew that it was for real. It was not just theory or head knowledge. It really was part of becoming *'mature, attaining to the whole measure of the fullness of Christ'* (Eph. 4:13-15). I actually thanked Him for trusting me, even with this experience, even if He never told me why.

A few days later I had occasion to ring up an elderly lady who lives near us. When she answered the phone, I knew at once that she was deeply distressed, almost unable to talk. I waited, listened, and then asked if I could help her at all. Suddenly, she burst out with a terrible story of how, a few nights previously, an intruder had entered her home and ransacked it while she was visiting her husband in hospital. At times she was almost incoherent with the overwhelming sense of the violation of her privacy and peace. Gently, I told her, 'I think I understand how this event has hurt you, and how you are now feeling. We also had an intruder only two weeks ago'. There was a startled silence. 'Did you really?' 'Yes,' I replied, and I told her a little bit of our 'event'. 'Oh, so you *do* understand how I feel!' she exclaimed. We talked for some twenty minutes as I sought to comfort her *'with the comfort we ourselves have received from God'* (2 Cor. 1:4).

Afterwards I thought, Isn't God good? He had prepared me for that moment so that I could comfort her meaningfully. Had we not suffered that shocking intrusion, I would not have been able to enter so wholeheartedly into that dear lady's distress. But how slow I am to learn! God has been teaching me this truth, by one means and another, over the past forty years. Despite that I had to fight to bring myself to say, 'Thank You, God, for trusting me with this experience, even if You never tell me why.' Another ditch was dug, and another blessing poured out by our gracious God.

Chapter Fourteen

A Return Home – Will this be the Start of another Ditch?

I sense that I may be nearing the end of this particular stretch of my life's journey – not that my valley is yet full of ditches, but that possibly God has a new direction for me. As a result, I find myself thinking in present tense and future possibilities, rather than past tense and memories. However, let me fill in a little background for this final chapter.

In September 1954, fifty years ago, I started work at Nebobongo, a small clearing in the Ituri forest in the northeastern province of what was then the Belgian Congo. With a willing team of African helpers, we embarked on the task of setting up a medical service for the church in the region for which our mission was responsible. There was already a brick-built maternity centre where Florence Stebbing cared for the women, and where she patiently trained Congolese girls to be midwives. There was no hospital. But there were some small buildings for the orphan children – mostly the children of leprous parents who had been segregated to protect them from infection – who were loved and cared for by five widowed ladies. It was decided to take over their buildings and re-house the little boys elsewhere in the village. Their dormitory became our operating theatre, scrub-up room, two small rooms for male and female changing, and another room for immediate post-operative care and office work. Indeed, this became our 'theatre' (O.R, to my American friends)!

It was in 1954 that I did my first-ever major operation there, a Caesarean section on a wee pigmy woman. The instruments I used were gifted by a widowed lady in the south of England after the death of her husband, who had been a surgeon. For the next fifty years that was the centre for all surgical procedures at Nebobongo Hospital, and many of those original instruments might still have been in use! Now it was to be all change!

Under the leadership of Dr Mola, with Mrs Mary Jean Robertson, a Canadian nurse, and a team of local workmen supervised by Berndt Lutz, a German engineer, a new complex for surgery was being constructed, new surgical instruments supplied, new equipment installed, and I was invited to go out to 'cut the tape' and dedicate the new facilities to the glory of God. It was an exciting, a thrilling, prospect! Dr Mola, our first Congolese doctor and a graduate of the University of Congo, has been in charge of the medical programme at Nebobongo for a few years, and has been very gracious in thanking me many times over for my part in establishing the medical service in our WEC area of responsibility in the D.R.Congo. He does not allow today's generation to forget that many of the present team of medical workers were trained at Nebobongo back in the 1950s and 1960s, and others at Nyankunde in the 1970s, when I had the privilege of being the doctor in charge of the teaching personnel. Now he suggested that it was time he and I met face to face!

Initially, Pat and I hoped to travel out there for Easter 2004, but the building was not ready due to all the 'unforeseen' frustrations and difficulties of any enterprise in the Ituri forest, which is hundreds of miles from stores and supplies, with roads increasingly impassable. Little by little the date was moved towards the end of the year. Eventually it was settled for mid-November. So what did God have for me to do in the months of waiting? There were weekly Bible studies at church, and with our girls on Sunday afternoons, a WEC holiday convention in Scotland at which we studied the biblical basis for true Christian fellowship in John's first letter, and the annual World Missions' Conference in Bangor. The days were full, and the Lord graciously filled us with His peace and joy.

At the Easter General Meeting of the members of our local church, I was invited to become the Church Treasurer, at least to fill in for a year. It sounded a simple enough task, taking note of all funds donated from whatever source, and paying the bills: heating, lighting, water, rates, office supplies, salaries of all staff, cleaners, and a hundred and one other expenses. But the struggle to make my accounts and monthly bank statements tally, to consistently make double-entries for all income and expenditure and to prepare simple monthly balance sheets to present intelligibly to the Church Committee combined to make me more and more aware of my personal insufficiency for the task!

As the weeks rolled relentlessly on, our proposed journey back to Africa drew nearer. I started reading my Bible aloud, every morning, in French and Swahili as well as in English, to get my ears accustomed again to the languages used at Nebobongo. Pat and I looked through our wardrobes to see that we had suitable cotton dresses, skirts and blouses. We began to think about what gifts we could take out to my dear friends, things that would neither add substantially to our weight nor cause difficulties at customs.

All injections and inoculations were completed and antimalarial medicine ordered. Odds and ends to take out to my many friends were gathering on our guest room bed … and there was only two weeks to go! The air tickets had been purchased, sterling currency exchanged for American dollars and suitcases brought down from the roof space. Anticipation was growing daily, and nervousness seemed to grow as fast!

****

We've been. We've returned. What a fantastic journey! What have we learned? How do we start to explain all that we saw and felt?

My friend Pat and I travelled out together and the journey was relatively straightforward, except that Pat's suitcase was left behind in London, half-filled with gifts to the Nebobongo Primary School children, and we did not meet it again until our homeward journey! The MAF plane met us in Entebbe International Airport, and took us into Congo, via a three-hour wait at Beni airstrip. Then it was on to Nebobongo on the edge of the great Ituri rain forest, arriving just before dusk to a rapturous welcome! School children, their parents, workmen, nurses – everyone waving and cheering and singing – and Doctor Mola and his brother Umo (the Senior Administrator of the medical service in our area) came forward to greet us. John Mangadima, my very first student in 1953, was there, as was Benjamin, my house-help all my years in Congo, and Mary-Jean Robertson, who was really responsible for all the arrangements and for our arrival. They were all there. We were led triumphantly the short walk up to the home that had been prepared for us for the week. I think we looked a little like the Pied Piper followed by an ever-growing excited crowd!

Outside the home, we found a welcome-banner of flowers and a row of cane chairs. And there was my dearest Congolese friend, Mama Taadi, frail and weak now, but with the same lovely smile and outstretched arms! We hugged each other ... and cried. It was just so good to be together again. My adopted daughter, Fibi, joined us. She is now a grandmother in her own rights! Then speeches began. The pastor spoke, then Dr Mola and Mangadima ... and I was expected to respond! How thrilled I was that the Swahili language returned to me as though I had never been away. I could understand everything they said, and they seemed well able to understand me.

A group of some twelve people gathered in front of us in the last glimmer of daylight. I recognised one of them, Bebesi, an excellent carpenter (really a cabinet maker) from the mid-fifties. Now lean, stooped and grey-haired, he had come to me in the first instance due to his having developed leprosy, as did so many of my early friends. The rest of the group had all been workmen or their wives from those early days. They started to sing to us. I could hardly believe my ears! They were singing the chorus that we had had in our Campaigner Clan, ending with the motto: 'Kwa Yeye, pasipo mupaka!' (Unto Him, through and through). They hadn't forgotten! I cried. It was so tremendous to realise that all the teaching and working of those long-ago days had borne fruit that was still evident.

During the next three days we were taken round the village to see all the improvements and changes. Permanent buildings of brick or cement blocks with corrugated iron roofing had largely replaced the mud-and-thatch hospital. Yet inside, the lack of beds, equipment and medicines was all too evident. Going to the south end of the village, we were welcomed by the primary school children – over 700 of them – with thirteen teachers, all standing on parade on the football field, and singing specially written songs in French and Swahili to greet us. Compared to the 120 children and four masters of the 1950s and 1960s, the growth was indeed impressive. But the eight classrooms, into each of which 55 or more children crowded each day for their classes, were still mostly mud-and-thatch with beaten earth floors and hardly any proper benches or desks. That was heartbreaking. [This is another of the projects close to Mary-Jean's heart – not just the hospital and new operating room, but new classrooms and furniture and equipment for the primary school.] The children are meant to pay a tiny sum each week for the right to be taught, but there is no money. So they arrive with a little bundle of firewood, or some other such offering for the teacher. The teachers receive practically no salary and the parents of the children have absolutely nothing with which to pay them. Yet their joy overflows. They sang to us so lustily. And as we walked into one, then another, of the classrooms we were amazed to see what was written on the blackboards. They were being well taught to a good standard.

We were then taken to the north side of the village, to see another primary school of some 300 children, and a secondary school, probably with about 120 children, in years one to four. These were private schools mainly for the children of the doctors, nurses, hospital and school staff. But how they were able to afford the slightly higher fees I never found out. It was a local initiative to keep these parents there at Nebobongo. Without proper schooling available for the children they would so easily have been tempted to leave, to seek work in one of the towns.

Everywhere there was this strange and disconcerting dichotomy. There was orderliness, discipline, good training and joy, but it was always alongside utter poverty, people with nothing of this world's goods, hardly enough even to live on. We came to the nurses' training school. The nurses too were all out on parade, as each of the other schools had been. There they were waiting for us, dressed immaculately in white, and singing in four-part harmony! Speeches were made, mostly in French, and that stretched me more than the Swahili. The nurses' school was better equipped than the primary schools, but their sleeping quarters were again unbelievably basic.

We were driven ten bone-shaking miles to the next village of Ibambi. This had always been the centre of the Mission's work, with its Bible School for training pastors for all the local churches, and a simpler Bible teaching centre for those who would assist those pastors, alongside its print shop, primary and secondary schools and a large church where 2-3,000 could crowd in for services. Again we were met by the whole population of the village, all singing and rejoicing to welcome us into their midst. We were escorted round to see various new initiatives, especially a centre set up by the Wycliffe Bible Translators to train national workers. And we went to see the cemetery, all beautifully cleaned and tended, where our founder, C.T. Studd, is buried along with some six other foreigners, several African pastors, and dear Mama

Anakesi, one of the very first nurse-midwives. In each place we visited, not only did they sing to us ecstatically but they also fed us – out of their poverty. Their extreme generosity was so moving that I was often almost in tears.

Then the BIG day arrived. They had erected a huge outdoor shelter with palm-frond covering, and from first light people began arriving from every direction carrying all kinds of seats, stools, chairs and benches, until eventually some 6-7,000 were there. An enormous procession slowly wound its way up the slight hill to the enclosure. There were nurses, technicians, workmen, bricklayers, a group of pygmies and the school children – nearly 2,000 altogether! And all the time we sang! Two choirs, duly robed, with drums as accompaniment, kept the proceedings moving. Then there were speeches from local government dignitaries and from Dr Mola, our Medical Superintendent, from the pastor and from Berndt, the German engineer who had overseen the building of the new operating theatre. After they had all spoken I was asked to bring the message to them all from the Word of God.

Eventually we were gently marshalled into order to process to the front of the new building. There was the tape, neatly prepared across the porch, and above it a sheet was hung. When we were all gathered the sheet was ceremoniously withdrawn, and the beautifully carved redwood sign was revealed to us all. Once again, I cried. In their hearts they were doing everything to honour *me* ... and I just wanted to crawl away and not be in the limelight. The new surgical unit was to be called by my African name, Mama Luka – the Surgical Centre of Mama Luka. They were humbly thanking me for having laid the foundations of today's work when I served there fifty years ago. The teaching programmes of today, so vastly superior to the small beginnings in 1954, were nevertheless seen by them to be a bringing in of the harvest of those early years of sowing and preparing the ground.

I was offered a beautiful new pair of surgical scissors on a presentation tray, with which to cut the tape. Prayer was offered, the tape was cut, and a short statement given that the building was now officially opened! And they cheered! There was an unbelievable welling up of happiness – a deep inner joy – a sense of the culmination of a long-held dream. For many it was really a moving forward into a future full of hope and anticipation with barely a thought about the difficulties, frustrations, shortages and poverty. It may also have been a drawing of a line under the past.

As I thought back over those fifty years, from being the only doctor (and I a foreigner) with Florence Stebbing, a nurse-midwife (and she also a foreigner) in charge of everything in every department in 1954, to 2004 with doctors, well-trained nurses, technicians, administrators, a pastoral care team – all nationals – all able to carry the work forward. It really was the fulfilment of a dream, a vision, that God had given me so long ago, when I first started work at Nebobongo, of seeing all the work led by Congolese.

Among other things we did in the days we had left was visit John Mangadima's village, some five miles along an almost impassable road into the forest, a road full of pot holes and ruts swirling with mud as torrential rain fell most days we were there. John had been appointed by the church leadership to become the pastor of the Anga Church. Once there he saw the need of the people for medical care, so he built a small hospital to run an efficient medical service for the local population, including surgery and maternity care. He also saw hundreds of primary school children, with no secondary education, so he built a secondary school and employed four or five qualified teachers for some sixty girls and boys! For sheer persistent, believing faith and initiative and determination, we had rarely seen anything comparable.

Everywhere we were feted and given flowers, presented with national dress and welcomed with songs and feasts, then offered amazing gifts. In one home we were offered four live chickens with their legs tied together. We had to accept their gifts, yet our hearts condemned us for accepting anything out of their appalling poverty. How could we refuse without hurting? 'Please, we do say a big big "Thank you!" for your love and your generosity to us, but would you allow us to give you back three of the hens?' we said, and they accepted them from us. Then a man, with an amazing story, came to the house where we were being fed. Fourteen months before our visit one of my dear friends, Mama Damaris, died, probably in her nineties. And she had made this man promise to keep her one goat, care for it, until 'we', her sisters, arrived, when he was to give it to us for a welcome feast. How could we refuse? Having kept the goat carefully all that time, he now brought it to us to fulfil his promise to dear Damaris. Such love!

At last the time came for us to leave Nebobongo. The little MAF plane came for us and, as we flew up over the forest and watched Nebobongo disappear in the distance, I began to feel a chapter had ended. But I wasn't yet sure ... We then flew to Nyankunde, to the other hospital where I worked from 1965 onwards. Over the years since then a large 250-bed hospital, with over 1,000 outpatients attending daily, and supporting a training college for some seventy two students annually, had come into being. And the College trained to a higher academic level than had been possible when we started at Nebobongo. When I left in 1973 there were several Western doctors and nurses there, and the standard of the training college was soon to rise to university status under the new leadership. Known as the Centre Medical Evangelique (CME in French, the Evangelical Medical Centre), Nyankunde became well known throughout not only Congo, but also Africa.

Then in 2002, inter-tribal fighting erupted in the district. In one terrible night the work of over thirty years was destroyed. Buildings were burned to the ground, ravished, wrecked. Possibly up to 2,000 were murdered, and there were other great brutalities and horrific atrocities. Patients, relatives, doctors and nurses were all victims. Others were enabled to escape, to flee on foot through the interminable forest to the south. After ten days of trekking they reached Oicha, another mission medical centre established by Dr Carl Becker, a renowned leprologist, who worked with the Africa Inland Mission back in the 1930s. We had a brief half hour to see something of the devastating destruction at Nyankunde, and the courage of a small group who were starting again in the burnt-out remains of the buildings.

From there we flew on to Oicha, where we saw a little of the enormous refugee camp on the one hand, and the continuing work of the hospital and nurses' training school on the other. Philip and Nancy Wood, two doctors who took over from me at Nyankunde when I had to leave in 1973, had returned to Oicha and were heading up the two wings of the ministry, the hospital with the College and the care of thousands of refugees and displaced people.

They had invited twelve or more of the 1967-1972 graduates from the Nyankunde School, when I was the doctor in charge of the training programme, to come and have an evening meal with us. After the meal (when we enjoyed a whole goat cooked on a spit!) three of the ladies, probably all in their 50s or 60s, stood up to sing to us – and they sang the first part of Handel's Hallelujah Chorus! We had learned it together all those years ago and they hadn't forgotten it! One of them imitated me as conductor, bringing in each of the voices in turn. It was hilarious! Deep inside me, along with the laughter there was a wonderful glow of comfort. God was so graciously showing me that those years – sometimes of hardship, often with frustrations, possibly loneliness – had not been in vain. How true '*Therefore, my dear brothers, stand firm. Let nothing move you. Always give yourselves fully to the work of the Lord, because you know that your labour in the Lord is not in vain*' (1 Cor. 15:58).

The following day we flew 25 miles to the south, to Beni, a large township with an airstrip, and with reasonable roads in all directions. Here Philip and Nancy had helped the medical staff to re-establish the 'Nyankunde CME' project in rented warehouses. We were greeted by the whole student body, all lined up in immaculate white uniforms, all singing in French, Swahili and even English, to welcome us. I was presented with a magnificent bunch of frangipani flowers, golden and white (actually, superb artificial silk flowers that I managed to bring home with me). We were led into their temporary chapel accommodation where the student body and the nursing staff of the hospital, including technical and practical workers, sang to us once again. I was invited to talk to them, which I was delighted to do. I shared the three 'musts' (oughts) from 1 John 2:6, 3:16 and 4:11. As Christian young people, privileged to be called into God's service, it is so essential that our whole lives bear testimony to His saving grace, not just our lips in what we say, but our behaviour and all we do. We *must* walk as Jesus walked, we *must* die to ourselves as Jesus died to Himself, and we *must* love one another as He loved us. They were so receptive, and their bright young faces thrilled me as I saw in them the hope of tomorrow for Congo.

We were shown all round their make shift hospital in the two warehouses that had been skilfully divided up by partitions into wards, clinics, laboratory, pharmacy, and all the other necessary departments for a modern teaching hospital. Then we were taken to see their sleeping accommodation. It was desperately cramped and with very little beyond basic essentials, but no one seemed to be complaining. They were just so grateful to God that they were alive, and that the staff was doing everything possible for them to continue their education.

At last we had to leave. Flying home, over the southern end of the Ruwenzori mountain range, the top of the mountain, which is over 16,000 feet high, was covered in clouds. I knew it was there, but it was hidden from view. Again, tears were very near as I thought how the future of Congo is indeed hidden to our view. All we hear is of warfare, rebel groups of soldiers ravaging and pillaging and harassing local populations, spreading fear and increasing poverty as they steal anything they see and want. Yet we know assuredly that there is a future for them. We have seen it in the shining faces of those young students. We have heard it in the confident voices of their church elders and pastors, and we have realised it in the persistent effort to rebuild every time their previous efforts are destroyed.

So we came home full of amazing memories, wonderfully encouraged to see the harvest of all the early years of preparing the soil, clearing out rocks and weeds, sowing the seed, watering … and waiting. And all that we had seen and heard engendered hope, hope to stand by them as they seek to go forward, to find a way to re-establish, not only the medical service and training schools, but even more the spiritual work among all age groups in every tribe throughout their vast country. Then came the niggling desire to go back again for a longer period. Could I be of service to them, perhaps just as a grandmother-figure, someone to listen, share, pray, and teach the Word, someone who could 'be available'? There were moments when this desire almost overwhelmed me, and I didn't want to back away if by any chance it was God's voice speaking to me. I asked Him to speak to me very clearly, to show me if this desire was His will for me.

Our daily reading at the time was in the final chapters of the first book of Chronicles. I came to chapter 17, when King David, settled in his beautiful palace, suddenly realises that the Almighty Lord God only had a tent. He wanted to build a dwelling place for the Ark of the Covenant, worthy of the Lord God. He was willing to give all he had to the task. But God spoke to the prophet Nathan, who came to King David with God's message full of promises of blessing, full of encouragement of peace and victory. Nathan said, '*You are not the one to build me a house to dwell in*' (1 Chron. 17:4). David responded in a prayer of thanksgiving and worship because God had brought him thus far, and was promising him so much for the future. '*There is no-one like you, O Lord, and there is no God but you!*' (17:20). He accepted that it would be his son, Solomon, who would build the temple for the Lord. So David set about preparing all that would be needed in the task: silver and gold, bronze and cedar timbers, iron and stone. In chapter 22, David said: '*My son Solomon is young and inexperienced, and the house to be built for the Lord should be of great magnificence and fame and splendour ...'* (22:5). Then he called his son and charged him to build the temple of the Lord God Almighty. *'Now, my son, the Lord be with you, and may you have success and build the house of the Lord your God, as He said you would'* (22:11).

As I read these chapters (including David's sin through pride, thinking he could do things for God in his own strength, and his repentance and God's forgiveness) I remembered so clearly the last time I talked and prayed with John Mangadima before I left Congo in 1973. I had explained these very same chapters to him, and then we turned together to chapter 28:9 through to the end of the chapter: *'And you, my son Solomon, acknowledge the God of your father, and serve him with wholehearted devotion and with a willing mind, for the Lord searches every heart and understands every motive behind the thoughts. If you seek him, he will be found by you; but if you forsake him, he will reject you for ever. Consider now, for the Lord has chosen you to build a temple as a sanctuary. Be strong and do the work!'* David then passed on to Solomon all the plans he had drawn up, and all the supplies he had amassed for the work. *'Be strong and courageous and do the work. Do not be afraid or discouraged, for the Lord my God is with you.'* I had prayed with John, 'passed him the keys', as it were, and left him in charge of the work that I had led for twenty years. Now the Lord chided me. 'You passed the responsibility on, now do you want to take it back? Can you not trust Me in them to complete the job?' Was I now jealous to get back into the task that had previously been assigned to me, but that had been handed on to the next generation? Did I think I could do it better than they could? Was I discontent with my present job description as a digger of ditches?

Maybe God has had to prise my hands off, like the folded-back sepals of the opening buttercup, never to close again, allowing Him to have His way. Surely I can rejoice in having been allowed by God, in His gracious mercy, to see so much of the fruit – the harvest – of all the early sowing, and to see the next generation taking over and carrying on the task so efficiently, without hankering to get back into the fray. 'I've given you another task now. Be content, and trust Me!' God seems to be saying to me.

So I trust my Congolese colleagues and friends into the Lord's hands, that He will keep them, lead them, and use them despite all the apparently insurmountable difficulties that surround them. And I must keep on digging ditches until my valley is full – without regrets, without looking backwards, but rather with joy and expectation, *waiting for the glorious appearing of our Great God and Saviour*.

Epilogue

~~~~~~

The Valley is Not Yet Full of Ditches!

'Make this valley full of ditches' (2 Kings 3:16).

For thirty years, that Bible verse has been my inspiration – the word from God to encourage me and keep me moving forward in His will.

'This valley' always speaks to me of the ever-present-tense nature of our God. He is the great 'I am' God (Ex. 3:14). 'My grace *is* sufficient for you!' (2 Cor. 12:9). God has taught me over many years to trust Him for today's needs and not to be hankering for the 'good old days' and looking backwards, nor to be planning endlessly for tomorrow and the 'what-might-be' of the future. He has taught me to believe utterly that He does know and understand my circumstances – including my needs, my hopes and my fears – and that His plan for my life takes all that into account, and brings peace. An acceptance of the fact that His will for my daily life is the best possible thing for me, does, in itself, bring peace.

The 'this valley' of thirty years ago, when God first spoke this verse into my heart, was different from the 'this valley' of today, but God is the same! Then there was the death of my dear mother and the uncertainty of my own health, the wrench of leaving Africa and the tension of trying to adapt to living in the affluent West. I had been asked to take on a roving deputation ministry for the Mission, with 'no fixed abode' as my residence. There was the realisation of endless travelling (and I suffered quite a lot from travel sickness!) and meeting up with new people every day when, basically, I am shy and not particularly outgoing. There was also the need to learn far more about the work and outreach of our Mission than just what was being done in Congo if I was to truly represent WEC to others, and I was very conscious of my own inadequacy for the task. Above all, the new calling in my life was open ended. There was no clear job description as there had been when I served as a doctor in Congo. And that caused me to fear. To whom was I ultimately responsible? I felt the need to be accountable to someone; but that was a very ill defined area in my appointment. It wasn't hard to see all of that as my 'this valley' when I started out in 1976.

But the truth of this Scripture has always to remain present tense. As the Lord graciously led me forward, step by step, to recognise those areas in my life that He wanted to change, and to allow Him to work through them with me, to bring about an ever-increasing trust in Him and therefore peace of heart, I came to see that my description of 'this valley' was bound to change.

My ability to keep abreast of changes in the Mission, and of the extent of the work in many countries and situations throughout the world, was no longer really sufficient for the task of representing them. Like others, as I grow older my memory is no longer as accurate as previously, and I am fearful that I will give facts wrongly. Travelling long distances across several time zones causes much more weariness as we get older than it does when we are young, and I dread becoming a burden to those whom I visit for ministry. Yet sitting at home and doing nothing is simply not an option! I long to be found working and watching for the Lord's coming again, not just waiting and watching. There is plenty to be done nearer home in our local church and amongst young people. Am I willing for continual daily direction as to the 'where' of service as well as to the 'what'? Is this perhaps an assessment of 'this valley' for me today? When the Lord shows a task that needs doing near home, is my temptation to think, 'That can't be for me. I'm no good at that!' or perhaps, 'surely so-and-so would be much more capable than me of doing that?' Or am I prepared to allow the Lord to help me to do what He asks me to do? Am I willing to think in terms of further training, or tackling a new task with new tools, and trusting Him to teach me the 'how' during the process?

'**Make**' is a verb of activity, not of sitting down and watching others! Yet, over the years, I believe that the emphasis has changed from the physical activity of 'doing' to, I trust, a more spiritual activity of 'becoming'. Early on, during my first years as a Christian, and also when I first arrived in Congo, I clung to the verse in John's Gospel, '*Whoever has my commands and obeys them, he is the one who loves me* (John 14:21). I have always been very hesitant about saying, or even believing, that I truly loved God. I knew I should, for all He has done for me and is to me, but did I actually love Him? When I was first saved, my understanding of the verb 'to love' was limited to what I had read in cheap and rather sloppy love stories and I did not have that sort of relationship with God. So the verse that said that my obedience to His commandments was in truth a demonstration of the fact that I loved Him was a great comfort to me, and I was willing to work round the clock to obey His commands. We used to say at Nebobongo, that we worked 25 hours in each day, 8 days every week, 53 weeks each year! And I loved it. I thrived on hard work, no matter how long the hours. I just wanted to show God – to tell Him – that I loved Him. It was my way of trying to say 'Thank You!' to Him for dying for me on the cross.

Slowly over many years, the Scriptures have shown me that although it is Biblically true that only obedience to His will can reveal our love for Him, the bottom line of His will for me is that I should become conformed to the image of His Son, that I should become Christlike. My enthusiasm for activity in my service for the Master – my 'making' the valley full of ditches – has to be tempered by an understanding that He is 'making' me come into line with His vision for my life. The Master Potter is moulding the jar of clay so that it can carry the Treasure (2 Cor. 4:7). How willing am I for the pressure of His hands moulding, refining, perfecting and making me into His vision for me? As I quoted from Oswald Chambers in chapter 13, it is not always what He is *teaching* me that is important, but rather, what He is *making* of me. My 'making this valley full of ditches' must, pre-eminently, come about as I allow God right of way in my heart and life, conforming me to the image of His Son.

Ditches – going back to the original story in Scripture, the ditches were to be dug by the soldiers in the sandy bed of the dried up River Arnon, so that God's gift of water would not be wasted, lost into the sand, but could be captured and used. Each soldier may have been ordered to dig a ditch, one metre long, 30 cm across, and 50 cm deep. How many thousands of soldiers might there have been? What a sight to see them all busy digging ditches, lines and lines of ditches! Where did they put the sandy soil that they dug out, without allowing it to fall into another man's ditch? It was not exactly the work for which they were trained, and they had not the right tools for it. But they were soldiers, and as such, they were expected to obey orders without questionings or murmurings. There was nothing to encourage them. The Lord had actually said: '*You will not see wind, nor rain*'. So why were they told to dig ditches? It was hot and tiring work. They had no water to drink. They must have felt very foolish. But as the day went on the number of ditches grew and grew.

Then in the night God filled the valley with precious, life-giving water. The ditches were filled. And in the morning everyone was able to slake their thirst, fill their water bottles, and bring their mules and other animals to drink. Furthermore, the rising sun shone down the valley from the east, and was reflected up as a red glow in the water. The enemy saw the redness and presumed it was the blood of rioting soldiers! They rushed down the mountainside to grab all the plunder they could, expecting no resistance from the Israelite army. But that army was ready for them and a great victory was won by God, due entirely to His gracious outpouring of blessing.

Ditches – God told me nearly thirty years ago that He wanted me to dig ditches, hundreds of little, often unconnected, ditches. Preaching, teaching, visiting, sharing, chatting, being available, in the main, without seeing any special blessing, these were the ditches I dug. They were the taking up of every opportunity of witnessing to God's love, by lip or by life, at meetings, in homes, sitting in an aeroplane or waiting in an airport; whether with students, senior citizens or primary school children; whether over the telephone or in a radio broadcast. I was not to question the where or the what of God's choice, but just to be ready and available to the Spirit, to buy up every opportunity. Each occasion was another ditch. God gave me no promise of hearing the rain or seeing the wind of His blessing. He just asked me for unquestioning obedience and absolute trust in Him with regard to the outcome.

In His grace, God has allowed me the huge encouragement – especially more recently – of hearing, every now and again, from someone who was especially blessed or heard the Lord's word of direction or came to know the next step they were to take in their lives at a particular meeting. Quite often, as they named or described the meeting, a wave of memory would come to me about how difficult I had found that occasion. Yet the Lord was at work, silently fulfilling His perfect purpose in this one life. God Himself had filled another 'ditch' with His own perfect blessing; the water of life had been given to another precious servant.

'Make this valley **full** of ditches!' But how do we know when the valley is full? How full of ditches does the valley have to be to be full? That reminds me of a youngster in our Nebobongo orphanage. As he was sent back from the line-up for lunch to wash his hands, he muttered as he turned away, 'How clean do my hands have to be to be clean?'

They are relative concepts, aren't they? Jaki's hands looked clean enough down in the shadows by the water hole, but in the full glare of the midday sunshine in the school courtyard, they looked anything but clean. The nearer we get to the sun, the more clearly we can see the dirt. The nearer we get to Jesus, the more clearly we realise the sinfulness and deceitfulness of our hearts. When compared to someone else's heart, my heart may look fairly good, or at least passable. But when compared to His utter purity, the truth is revealed and I am in no doubt of my need of His gracious cleansing.

Is it the same with being 'full'? The widow, told to bring empty jars and to pour out her meagre supply of oil, had enough oil to fill every jar until she ceased to bring another empty one. Then the oil stopped flowing. When Elisha told King Joash to shoot an arrow out of the window, it was to be the sign of Israel's victory over Syria. Then Elisha told the king to strike the ground with the arrows, and the king struck just three times and stopped, and Elisha was angry with him for stopping! *'You should have struck the ground five or six times, then you would have defeated Aram and completely destroyed it. But now you will defeat it only three times'* (2 Kings 13:19). Is the temptation to want to stop 'digging ditches' and perhaps do something apparently more interesting, more fruitful, and more meaningful in the public eye? Yet the question is still there, Is the valley *full* of ditches yet?

May the Lord give me stickability to persevere with the task until it is completed, and not to ask for a new word of direction whilst there is still leeway in the fulfilment of the previous clear word. Did the Lord God not promise that His Spirit would speak a word in our ears saying: *'This is the way; walk in it'* whenever we turn out of the way, to the right or the left? (Is. 30:21). Surely this indicates that He has no need to speak such a word into our hearts when we keep in the way! We are just to keep on keeping on, with our eyes fixed on Jesus, the Founder and Perfecter of our faith (Heb.12:2). He will indeed hold our hand and guide us through the dark places as well as those that are full of light, the difficult as well as the relatively easy, the sad as much as the joyous. He has promised, *'Never will I leave you; never will I forsake you'* (Heb.13:5), but rather, that He will be with us to the end – to the end of the world, to the end of time, to the end of our sense of need! Wonderful Lord and Saviour!

May I be kept willing to obey His sure word to me:

'Make this valley full of ditches!'

Miracles from Mayhem

The Story of May Nicholson

Irene Howat

'May has the same love for the poorest of the poor and the richest of the rich. She is at home with lords and ladies and with the lowly and loneliest. Living out God's love with and among the poor, she reflects Jesus who, "though he was rich, yet for yoursake he became poor that we might be made rich.'

Chuck Wright

'Anyone who has lived with drug addicts and alcoholics knows how elusive hope is. It runs through your fingers like fine sand, until there's nothing left but cynicism and despair. But May Nicholson found a different sort of hope – rather, it found her! Her encounter with Jesus Christ literally "saved" her life, and set in motion what one of her colleagues calls 'a friendly steamroller' – clearing paths of hope not just for herself but for dozens and dozens of others too.'

John Nicholls, London City Mission

May Nicholson was a notorious fighting drunk until her conversion when she was 34. The last 22 years have been spent tirelessly working for the Lord as an outreach worker in Paisley, Dundee and Glasgow's Govan.

This book tells a remarkable story of a life completely changed and transformed by God.

Irene Howat, an award winning author, has also written 'Whitewashed Stairs to Heaven' ISBN 1-85792-616-1 and 'Light in the City' ISBN 1-85792-723-0.

ISBN 1-85792-897-0

Mission to the Headhunters

How God's Forgiveness Transformed Tribal Enemies

Frank and Marie Drown

'*The book is straightforward and beauti-fully written. It's a page-turner. I was stag-gered and rebuked, helped and cheered by the steadfast faithfulness of this humble (I'm sure they would say merely ordinary) couple. Read it!*'

Elisabeth Elliot Gren,
Author of "Through Gates of Splendor"
Radio Host of "Gateway to Joy"

'*What an incredible story of the Lord building His church... Don't miss reading about this challenge of the century!*'

The Late Carl McMindes, Formerly President,
Gospel Missionary Union, Kansas City, Missouri

'*Few people know missions from the inside out the way Frank and Marie Drown do. Mission to the Headhunters captures their com-mitment and passion for reaching a lost world with the Gospel. The message of this book is greatly needed by today's generation.*'

Don Hawkins, President,
Southeastern Bible College, Birmingham, Alabama

Frank and Marie were missionaries in Ecuador for thirty-seven years. During that time they saw huge changes as they reached the Indians with the Gospel. This is their remarkable story.

ISBN 1-85792-721-4

Christian Focus Publications
publishes books for all ages
Our mission statement –

STAYING FAITHFUL

In dependence upon God we seek to help make His infallible Word, the Bible, relevant. Our aim is to ensure that the Lord Jesus Christ is presented as the only hope to obtain forgiveness of sin, live a useful life and look forward to heaven with Him.

REACHING OUT

Christ's last command requires us to reach out to our world with His gospel. We seek to help fulfill that by publishing books that point people towards Jesus and help them develop a Christ-like maturity. We aim to equip all levels of readers for life, work, ministry and mission.

Books in our adult range are published in three imprints.

Christian Focus contains popular works including biographies, commentaries, basic doctrine and Christian living. Our children's books are also published in this imprint.

Mentor focuses on books written at a level suitable for Bible College and seminary students, pastors, and other serious readers. The imprint includes commentaries, doctrinal studies, examination of current issues and church history.

Christian Heritage contains classic writings from the past.

Christian Focus Publications, Ltd
Geanies House, Fearn,
Ross-shire, IV20 1TW, Scotland, United Kingdom
info@christianfocus.com

For details of our titles visit us on our website
www.christianfocus.com